Apple Watch Series 5 Users Manual

Complete and Illustrated Guide with Tips and Tricks to Operate Your iWatch Series 5 Like a Pro

Nobert Young

Copyright @ 2020

Table of Content

Introduction 12

Chapter 1: Set Up the Apple Watch 13

   Power On Apple Watch 13

   Automatically Pair Apple Watch with your iPhone 13

   Set Up Apple Watch From Scratch 14

   Restore Apple Watch From a Backup 18

   Manually Pair Apple Watch with iPhone 21

   Unpair Apple Watch 22

   Erase Your Apple Watch 23

   Pair Multiple Apple Watches to One iPhone 25

   Quickly Switch to a Different Apple Watch 25

   Disable Automatic Watch Switch 26

   Manually Switch Between Apple Watches 26

   Transfer Watch to a Different iPhone 27

   Update Your Apple Watch on Watch App 29

   Update on the Apple Watch 29

Chapter 2: Apple Watch with Cellular Plan 31

   Set Up Cellular Plan 31

   Changing Carriers 31

   Remove Cellular Plan 31

   Transfer Cellular Plan to a New Watch 32

Chapter 3: Wi-fi 33

   Select a Wi-Fi Connection 33

   Disconnect from Wi-fi 33

   Forget a Wi-fi Network 34

Chapter 4: Passcode 35
   Add Passcode from iPhone 35
   Create Passcode on Apple Watch 35

Chapter 5: Listen to Music 36
   Add Music to Apple Watch 36
   Add Playlists and Albums to Apple Watch 37
   Add a Workout Playlist 38
   Sync Music to Your Apple Watch 38
   See How Much Music You Have on Your Watch 39
   Remove Music From Apple Watch 39
   Listen to Music from Music Library 40
   Play Music From iPhone 41
   Listen to Apple Music 41
   Open the Up Next Queue 42

Chapter 6: Podcasts and AudioBooks 43
   Sync Podcasts to Your Apple Watch 43
   Sync Audiobooks 44
   Add a Workout Podcasts 45
   Listen to Podcasts Stored on the Watch 46
   Play Podcasts from iPhone 46
   Play Podcast from Your Library 47
   Play Podcasts with Siri 47

Chapter 7: The Workouts App 48
   Start a Workout 48
   Pause Workout 49
   End Workout 50

Lock Workout 51

Track Your Progress 51

Set Target Pace for Outdoor Runs 52

Combine Multiple Activities in a Single Workout 53

Change Workout Metrics 54

Add a Workout 55

Listen to Music During a Workout 56

Reminder to Start a Workout 56

Get Reminders to End Your Workout 57

Save Power During Workouts 58

Enable Running Auto Pause 60

View Workout Activity 61

View Your Activity History 63

View Workout History 63

View Activity Trends 63

Share Activity Data 64

Start a Competition on iPhone 66

Start a Competition on Apple Watch 66

Compare Activity Data on Apple Watch 67

Compare Activity Data on iPhone 67

Complete a Challenge 68

Hide Your Progress 68

Remove a Friend 69

Chapter 8: The Breathe App 70

Start a Breathe Session 70

Customize Breathing Reminders 70

Set Duration of a Breathe Session. 70

View Heart Rate During Breathe Sessions 71

Chapter 9: Heart Rate on Apple Watch 72

Monitor Your Heart Rate 72

Check Your Heart Rate During a Workout...73

View A Graph of Your Heart Rate Data.. 74

Enable Heart Rate Data 74

Enable High or Low Heart Rate Notification.. 74

Set Up Irregular Heart Rhythm Notification 75

View Irregular Rhythm Notification Data 76

View Your Health Information 77

Chapter 10: ECG on Apple Watch... 79

Set Up the ECG App 79

Take an ECG 81

View and Share ECG Data on the Health App.. 82

Chapter 11: Fall Detection.. 84

Enable or Disable Fall Detection 84

Set Up Your Medical ID... 86

Edit Emergency Contacts 87

Make an Emergency Call.. 88

End the Call... 89

Call Emergency Services 89

Stop Sharing Your Location... 90

Disable Automatic Dialing 90

Chapter 12: Track Your Sleep on Apple Watch.. 92

Download Sleep Tracker... 92

Chapter 13: The Noise App 97
Set Up the Noise App on the Apple Watch 97
Enable/ Disable Noise Notification on iPhone 97
Monitor Noise on the Apple Watch 98
View Information about Environmental Sound Levels 98
Disable or Enable Noise Measuring 99

Chapter 14: Cycle Tracking 100
Setup Cycle Tracking on iPhone 100
Track Your Menstrual Cycles 101

Chapter 15: Basic Settings 102
Power Off Apple Watch 102
Force restart Your Watch 102
Unlock Your Mac with Apple Watch 102
Change Apple Watch Bands 104
View Your Calendar Events 104
Set Default City for the Weather App 106
Organize Your App 106

Chapter 16: Walkie- Talkie on Apple Watch 107
Enable or Disable Walkie-Talkie 107
Add Friends to the App 107
Remove a Friend 108
Accept Walkie-Talkie Invitation 108
Start a Walkie-Talkie Conversation 109

Chapter 17: Find My 110
Find Your iPhone with Apple Watch 110
Find Your Apple Watch 110

Mark Apple Watch As Lost 111

Chapter 18: Camera App 112

Take a Photo 112

Remotely Take a Photo on Your Phone 112

Take a Live Photo 112

Use a Different Camera 113

Use a Different Camera Mode 113

View Your Shots on Apple Watch 114

Chapter 19: Photo App 115

Browse Photos 115

View Photos on the Photos App 115

View Life Photo on Apple Watch 116

Show a Photo on The Watch Face 116

Limit Photo Storage on Apple Watch 116

View Number of Photos Stored on Your Watch 116

Take a Screenshot 117

Chapter 20: Apple Watch App Store 118

Customize App Store Settings on Apple Watch 118

Customize App Store Settings on iPhone 118

View App Details 119

Download Apps to the iPhone and Watch Simultaneously 120

App Store on Apple Watch 120

View Purchased Apps 122

Delete Apps from Watch 122

Chapter 21: Apple Pay 124

Set Up Apple Pay 124

Choose Default Card 124

Remove a Card From Apple Pay 125

Pay With the Apple Watch 125

Find Device Account Number for a Card 126

Modify Default Transaction Details 126

Chapter 22: Siri 127

Set Up Siri 127

Enable Raise to Speak 127

Manually Activate Siri 128

Hey Siri 128

Change Siri's Voice on Apple Watch 128

Disable Siri Voice on Apple Watch 129

Use Handoff to Switch From Siri on Your Watch to Your Phone 130

Set Up Siri Watch Face 131

Set Up Siri Watch Face on iPhone 132

Use Siri Watch Face 133

Chapter 23: Watch Faces 134

The Face Gallery 134

Add Complications on the Apple Watch 134

Add Complications from Other Apps 135

Install a New Watch Face 136

View Your Watch Face Collection 136

Change Watch Faces 137

Create Watch Faces with Photos 137

Delete Watch Faces Via iPhone 138

Delete a Face From Your Collection 139

Make Your Watch Five Minutes Fast 140

Chapter 24: Control Your Home with Apple Watch 141

Add a New Scene or Accessory 141

Control Smart Home Accessories 141

Control Smart Home Scenes 142

View a Different Home 142

Chapter 25: Screen Display 143

Show Last Used App on Wake Screen 143

Enable Always on Display 144

Wake the Watch Display 145

Disable Wake Screen on Wrist Raise 145

Keep the Watch Display Longer 145

Enable Flashlight 146

Theater Mode on Apple Watch 146

Change Brightness and Text Size 147

Chapter 26: Sounds and Notifications 149

Enable Silent Mode 149

Disable Silent Mode on Watch App 149

Mute Alerts with Your Palm 149

Enable Do Not Disturb 149

Set Up Notifications 150

View Notifications 151

Clear Notifications Quickly 151

Hide Notifications 152

Disable Notifications on iPhone and Apple Watch 152

Disable Notifications for Third-Party Apps 153

Chapter 27: Accessibility on Apple Watch 155
Set Side Button Speed 155
Enable VoiceOver on Apple Watch 155
Enable VoiceOver Via Watch App 155
Enable Zoom on Apple Watch 156
Enable Zoom Via Watch App 157
Control Zoom on Apple Watch 157
Customize Accessibility Shortcut 158

Chapter 28: Time Keeping 159
Set an Alarm 159
Delete an Alarm 159
See the Same Alarms on Apple Watch and iPhone 160
Disable Snooze on Apple Watch 160

Chapter 29: Messages and Communication 161
Pre-Compose Custom Message Responses 161
Send Dictated Text as Audio 162
Share Your Location in Messages 162
Call the Person You Are Messaging 163
Hold a Call Until You Can Find Your iPhone 163
Send Money With Apple Pay 163
Cancel a Payment 164
Request a Payment 164
Respond to Payment Request 164
Create a Message on Apple Watch 164
Reply to a Message 165
Scribble a Message 165

Send Emoji 166

Send Animoji/ Memoji in the Messages App 166

Choose the Mailboxes that Should Appear on Your Watch 167

Flag a Mail 167

Chapter 30: The Dock on your Apple Watch 168

Use Dock to Switch Between Apps 168

Select Apps that Should Appear in the Dock 168

Add Favorite Apps to the Dock 168

Add Apps to Your Watch Dock 169

Rearrange Apps in Your Dock 170

Remove Apps From Your Dock 170

Chapter 31: Water Lock Mode 172

Enable Water Lock 172

Eject Water 172

Chapter 32: Free Up Space on Your Watch 174

Check Storage Space on Apple Watch 174

Check Storage Space on iPhone 175

Remove Apps From Watch App 176

Delete Apps on Apple Watch 177

Remove Music From Watch App 178

Delete Music on Apple Watch 179

Resync Photos from Watch App 180

Remove Audiobooks 181

Remove Podcasts 182

Chapter 33: Battery Tips 184

Enable Power Reserve Mode 184

Disable Power Reserve Mode 184
　　Check Battery Percentage 184
Conclusion **185**
Other Books By Nobert Young **186**

Introduction

The Apple Watch Series 5 was announced on September 10, 2019, and became available on September 20. The main selling feature of the smartwatch is the Always-on display - whenever you look at your wrist, you will view your time and other configured details on your watch screen. The watch is also the first to have a built-in compass.

The watch is available in the LTE model, as well as the GPS model. The watch may not be as big and powerful as the iPad or iPhone, but it has so much packed into its small package.

There are a lot of activities that you can perform on your watch, including tracking your workouts, listening to music, viewing your photos, reading ECG, answering calls, contacting emergency services, and monitoring your heart rate. And just like you have on the iPad and iPhone, the Apple Watch has different options and settings that you need to tweak to make the watch work and act the way you desire.
In this user guide, you will find all the tips and tricks you need to get the best from your Apple Watch.

Chapter 1: Set Up the Apple Watch

The first step to enjoying your Apple Watch is to pair it with your iPhone. You will be unable to fully operate the Apple Watch without depending on the iPhone for some settings.

Power On Apple Watch

To power on the watch, press down the side button until you see the Apple logo on your screen.

Automatically Pair Apple Watch with your iPhone

After you power on your Apple Watch for the first time, the next step is to pair the watch with your iPhone.

- Open the Watch app on your iPhone or bring your Apple Watch close to the iPhone and tap **Continue** on your watch screen to launch the Watch App. Click on **Start Pairing** on the iPhone.

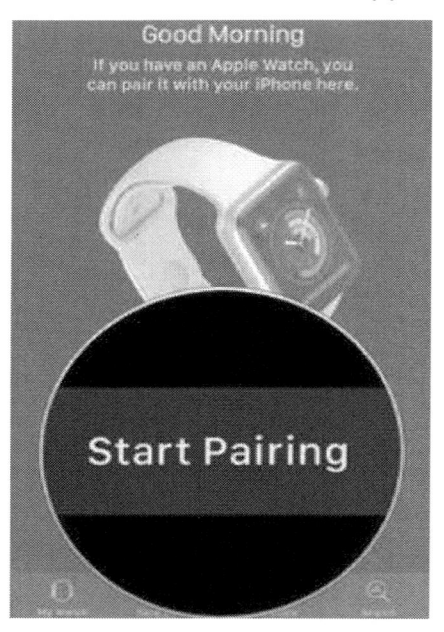

- Place the camera of your iPhone over the watch until the watch screen fills the rectangle on the iPhone screen.

- Once successfully paired, you will get the message "**Your Apple Watch Is Paired.**"
- Click on the option to **Restore Apple Watch from a Backup** or to **Set Up as New Apple Watch.**
- Then follow the steps below to complete the setup.

Set Up Apple Watch From Scratch

After pairing the Apple watch with the steps above, follow the steps below to set up your Apple Watch from scratch.

- At the end of the pairing process, click on **Set Up as New Apple Watch**.
- Select either **Right** or **Left** to choose the wrist that you plan to wear the smartwatch on.
- **Agree** to the displayed terms and conditions.
- Click on **Agree** again.
- If prompted, enter your Apple ID and password to activate **Find My** and **Activation Lock.**
- Click on **OK** to confirm you understand the shared settings between your Apple Watch and the iPhone.
- Click on **Create a Passcode** to set up a 4-digit passcode for your watch. To set a passcode that is longer than four digits, tap **Add a Long Passcode, t**hen input the desired passcode on the screen

of the Apple Watch. Click on **Don't Add Passcode** to skip this step.

- For Apple Watch with cellular service, click on **Set Up Cellular** to set up Cellular service. Then follow the steps on your phone screen. Tap **Continue** to proceed with the setup. Tap **Skip This Step** to set up cellular at a later time.

- Tap **Continue** to set up Apple Pay or click on **Set Up Later** to do this at a later time.
- Tap **Continue** to agree with Emergency SOS.

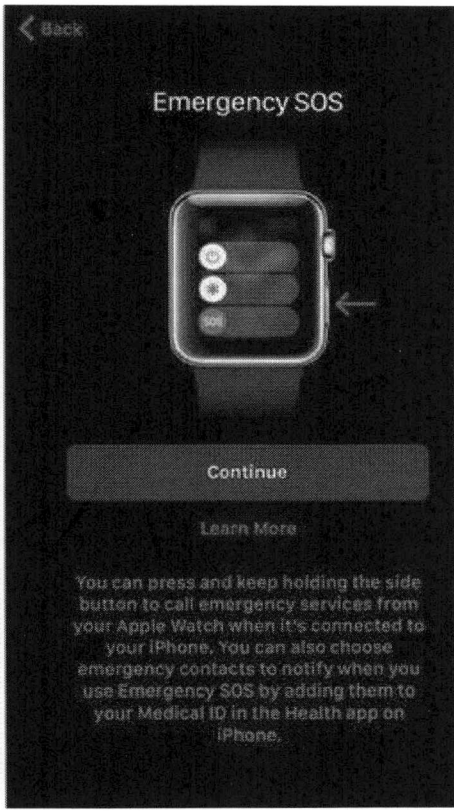

- Click on **Install All** to get all the available watch apps on your iPhone or click on **Choose Later** to do this at a later time.
- Wait for the watch to sync with your paired iPhone. And then, the watch is ready for use.

Restore Apple Watch From a Backup

Use this setup option if you have an existing Apple Watch and will like to transfer data from the old watch to the new one.

- At the end of the pairing process, click on **Restore from Backup**.

- Click on the desired backup.
- **Agree** to the displayed terms and conditions.
- Click on **Agree** again.
- If prompted, enter your Apple ID and password to activate **Find My** and **Activation Lock.**
- Click on **OK** to confirm you understand the shared settings between your Apple Watch and iPhone.
- Click on **Create a Passcode** to set up a 4-digit passcode for your watch. To set a passcode that is longer than four digits, tap **Add a Long Passcode t**hen input the desired passcode on the screen of the Apple Watch. Click on **Don't Add Passcode** to skip this step.

- Re-enter the password one more time to confirm.
- For Apple Watch with cellular service, click on **Set Up Cellular** to set up Cellular service. Then follow the steps on your phone screen. Tap **Continue** to proceed with the setup. Tap **Skip This Step** to set up cellular at a later time.

- Tap **Continue** to set up Apple Pay or click on **Set Up Later** to do this at a later time.
- Tap **Continue** to agree with Emergency SOS.

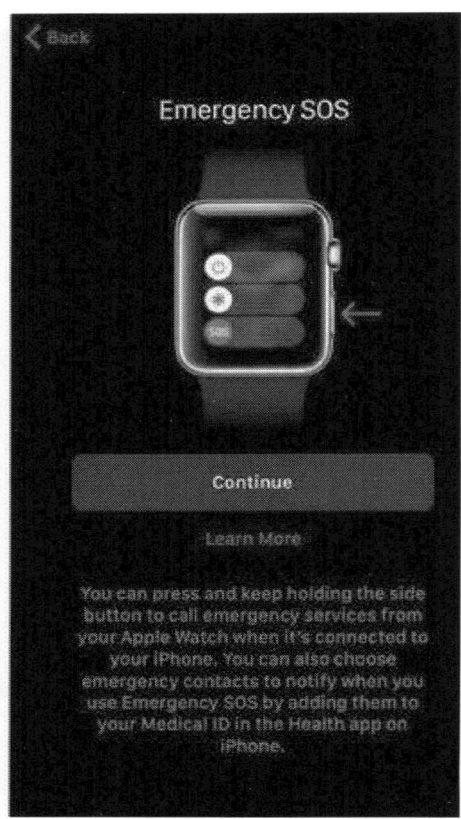

- Your watch will then begin to restore the backup. Once the backup is complete, you can start using your watch.

Manually Pair Apple Watch with iPhone

If the Apple watch failed to pair with your iPhone automatically, follow the steps below to pair it manually.

- Open the Watch app on your iPhone or bring your Apple watch close to the iPhone to launch the Watch App.
- Click on **Start Pairing.**
- Then click on **Pair Apple Watch Manually.**

- Tap ⓘ on your watch screen to get the name of your watch.
- Then click on the Apple Watch from the displayed list on your iPhone.

- Click on the option to **Restore Apple Watch from a Backup** or to **Set Up Your Watch From Scratch.**

Unpair Apple Watch

You may choose to unpair your watch from one iPhone and pair it with another phone. If you want your watch data backed up, you will need to perform the unpair process using the Watch app on your iPhone.

- Open the Watch app on your phone and click on **My Watch** at the bottom of your screen.

- Then click on your Apple Watch at the top side of your screen.
- Tap ⓘ beside the watch you want to unpair, then click on **Unpair Apple Watch**.
- Click on **Unpair (Watch Name)**.
- Select either **Remove** or **Keep** for your cellular plan.
- On the next screen, enter your Apple ID and click on **Unpair**.
- Wait for your phone to back up your watch's latest data and complete the unpairing process.

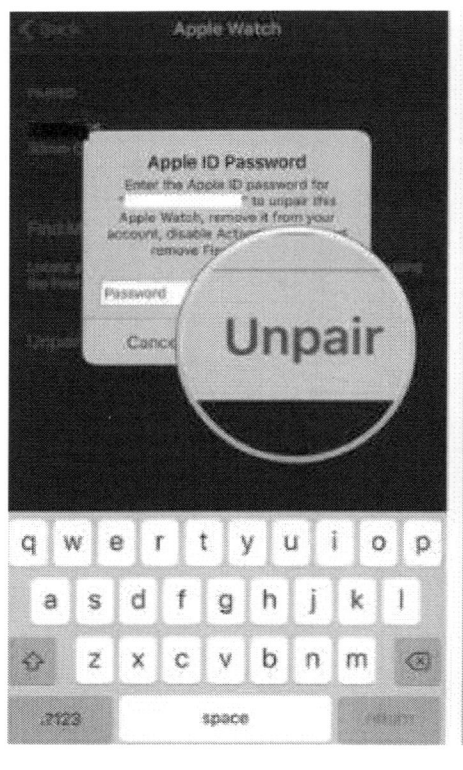

Erase Your Apple Watch

For some reasons, you may experience difficulties unpairing the watch using the iPhone. These reasons may be that the iPhone is no longer in your possession or not available at the time you need to perform the unpairing process. Erasing your apple watch will return it to its default setting and will cause you to lose your watch data. However, it makes the watch available for pairing with another iPhone.

- Open the Settings app on your Watch and click on **General**.
- Then click on **Reset**.

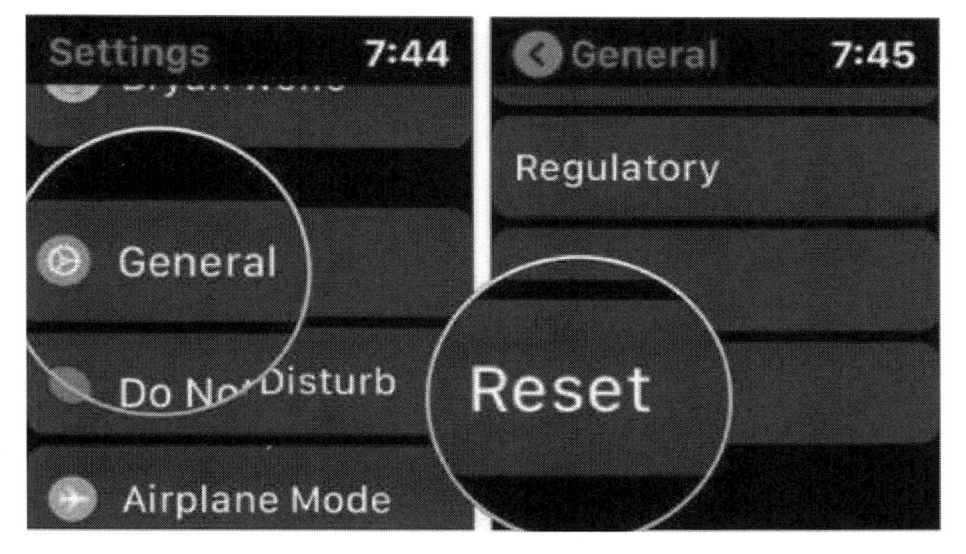

- Click on **Erase All Content and Settings**.
- Enter your passcode if you have one.
- Then click on **Erase All**. To retain your cellular plan, click on **Erase All & Keep Plan**.
- Once this is done, visit iCloud.com from your web browser to disable Activation Lock.
- Enter your Apple ID and password, then click on **Settings**.

- Navigate to **My Devices** and click on your Apple Watch.
- Click on the **X** button by the right side of the watch to remove it.
- Then click on **Remove** to complete your action.

Pair Multiple Apple Watches to One iPhone

You can pair more than one Apple Watch to your iPhone in two methods

Method 1:
- Follow the pairing method you used for the first Apple Watch, as detailed above.

Method 2:
- Open the Watch app on your phone and click on the **My Watch** tab at the bottom of your screen.
- Click on the current Apple Watch at the top of your screen.
- Then click on **Pair New Watch** and follow the instructions on your screen to complete.

Quickly Switch to a Different Apple Watch

If you have two Apple watches paired to your iPhone, you can quickly switch between the Apple watches. To do this, take off the first watch, wear the second watch, then move your arm or raise your wrist to complete the switch.

Disable Automatic Watch Switch

If you do not want the system to automatically switch your paired watches when you wear a different watch, you can disable the automatic switch with the steps below:
- Open the Watch app on your phone and click on **My Watch** at the bottom of your screen.
- Click on your Apple Watch at the top side of your screen.
- Toggle off **Auto Switch.** Toggle on this option if you want to use the **Automatic Switch.**

Manually Switch Between Apple Watches

If you disabled Auto switch above, you could manually switch between two apple watches with the steps below:

- Open the Watch app on your phone and click on **My Watch** at the bottom of your screen.
- Click on your Apple Watch at the top of your screen.
- Then click on the second watch that you want to switch to. You will see this checkmark beside the selected Apple watch.

Transfer Watch to a Different iPhone

WatchOS does not support sharing one watch across multiple iPhones. If you got a new phone and want to pair your watch to the phone, you will need to first unpair the watch from the old phone using the steps listed in the **Unpair** section, then follow the steps below to complete the set up without losing your data.

Note that both the new phone and the Apple watch needs to be at least 50% charged. The new and the old iPhone also has to be connected to Wi-Fi.

- Update your old iPhone and your Apple Watch.
- Check that your activity and health settings are enabled. To do this, open the Settings app on your old phone, click on your name at the top of the screen, click on iCloud, then confirm that **Health** is toggled on.
- Then back up your old iPhone.
- Power on and set up your new iPhone. During the setup, your phone may ask if you want to use your Apple Watch. Tap

Continue to proceed. If the phone doesn't ask, continue to the next step below.

- Open the Watch app on your new phone. Let your watch be close to the new phone. You will receive a prompt to confirm if you want to set up the Apple Watch. Follow the pairing process in this book or follow the instructions on your screen to successfully pair your watch with the new phone.

If you do not have the old iPhone but need to pair your watch with the new iPhone, follow the steps below:

- **Erase your Apple watch** with the steps contained in this book.
- Set up your new iPhone.
- Open the Watch app on your new phone. Place your smartwatch close to the new phone. You will receive a prompt to confirm if you want to set up the Apple Watch. Follow the pairing process in this book or follow the instructions on your screen to successfully pair your watch with the new phone.

Update Your Apple Watch on Watch App

Whenever there is a new update, you will receive a prompt on your watch, notifying you of the update. Open the notification and click on **Update Tonight,** then switch to your paired iPhone and confirm that you want to update the watch overnight. Connect the phone and watch to power through the night to complete the automatic update.

To manually check for updates,

- Open the Watch app on your phone and click on **My Watch** at the bottom of your screen.
- Click on **General,** then click on **Software Update.**

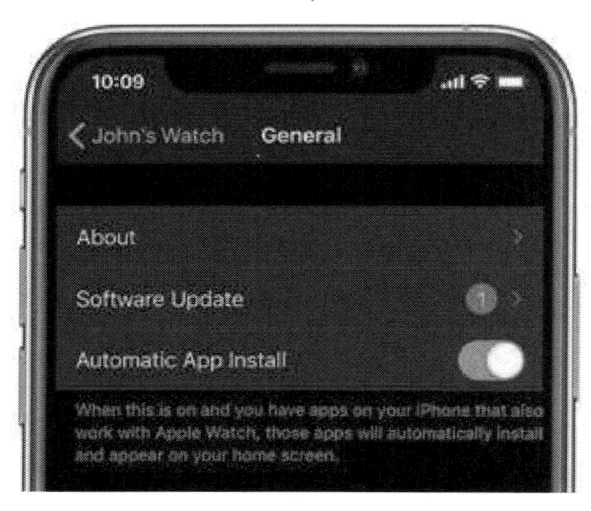

- Click on the update to download it. Enter your passcode if prompted.

Update on the Apple Watch

- Open the Settings app on your watch and click on **General.**

- Click on **Software Update,** then click on the available update and follow the steps on your screen to complete the update.

Chapter 2: Apple Watch with Cellular Plan

The cellular connection on your watch allows you to reply to messages, make calls, receive notifications, and several other features, even without the iPhone being nearby.

Set Up Cellular Plan

Follow the steps below to set up a cellular plan on your watch:
- Launch the Watch app on your phone and click on **My Watch.**
- Click on **Cellular,** then click on **Set Up Cellular** and follow the instructions on your screen.

Changing Carriers

You have to use the same carrier for both the iPhone and the watch. If you change the carrier on your iPhone, you will also need to update the change on your watch. See how to update your carrier on the watch:
- Launch the Watch app on your iPhone and click on **My Watch.**
- Click on **Cellular,** and the watch will automatically switch to the carrier on your paired phone.
- To add a new plan, click on **Add A New Plan,** then follow the instructions on your screen.

Remove Cellular Plan

You may choose not to use the cellular option on your watch. To remove an active cellular plan,
- Launch the Watch app on your phone and click on **My Watch.**
- Click on **Cellular,** then click on ⓘ beside the plan at the top of your screen.

- Click on **Remove (Carrier) Plan** and confirm your action.

Transfer Cellular Plan to a New Watch

Here is how to transfer a cellular plan from one watch to another.

- The first step is to remove the cellular plan from the current watch. Follow the steps above to remove the plan from your old watch.
- Pair the new watch with your iPhone:
  - Open the Watch app on your iPhone or bring your Apple Watch close to the iPhone and tap **Continue** on your watch screen to launch the Watch App. Click on **Start Pairing** on the iPhone.
  - Place the camera of your iPhone over the watch until the watch screen fills the rectangle on the iPhone screen.
- Once successfully paired, you will get the message "**Your Apple Watch Is Paired.**"
- Click on **Set Up Cellular** during the setup process to include a cellular plan.

Chapter 3: Wi-fi

Select a Wi-Fi Connection

- Press the digital crown one time to go to the home screen.
- Tap the icon to open the Settings app.
- Toggle on **Wi-Fi.**
- Your watch will start to search for available networks. Click on the network you wish to join.
- Scribble your password if prompted, then tap **Join.**

Disconnect from Wi-fi

You can choose to use cellular connection rather than a Wi-fi network on your watch.

- Swipe up on the Apple watch face to open the Control Center.
- Tap the wi-fi icon to disable wi-fi. Click the same icon to enable wi-fi.

- Swipe down from the top of your screen to exit control center.

Forget a Wi-fi Network

- Press the digital crown one time to go to the home screen.
- Tap the icon to open the Settings app.
- Click on **Wi-Fi.**
- Click on the wi-fi network you wish to forget.
- Then tap **Forget This Network** to complete.

Chapter 4: Passcode

Add a passcode on your watch to give your device an added layer of security.

Add Passcode from iPhone

- Launch the Watch app on your phone and click on **My Watch.**
- Click on **Passcode,** then click on **Turn Passcode On.**
- When prompted, enter the new four-digit passcode on the screen of your Apple Watch. Re-enter the passcode to confirm.
- Now return to your iPhone screen. To set a passcode that is longer than four digits, enable **Simple Passcode.** Enter your recently created passcode to proceed.
- You will then receive a prompt to set the new passcode.
- Return to your watch screen to enter the new passcode.

Create Passcode on Apple Watch

To create your passcode right on the Apple Watch,

- Press the digital crown one time to go to the home screen.
- Tap the ![icon] icon to open the Settings app.
- Click on **Passcode**. Click on **Turn Passcode On.**
- When prompted, enter a four-digit passcode on your Apple Watch. Re-enter the passcode to confirm.
- To set a passcode that is longer than four digits, toggle on **Simple Passcode.** Enter your recently created passcode to proceed.
- You will then receive a prompt to set the new passcode.

Chapter 5: Listen to Music

Add Music to Apple Watch

Add music to your watch and listen to them even when you do not have your iPhone close. You can choose the playlists that should be added automatically to your Watch. This offer is for Apple Music subscribers. Apple Music automatically adds personalized mixes to your Watch whenever it is connected to power. The steps below will show you how to change the playlists that are automatically added:

- Launch the Apple Watch app on your iPhone.
- Click on **My Watch** at the bottom of your screen, then click on **Music.** Disable or enable individual playlists.

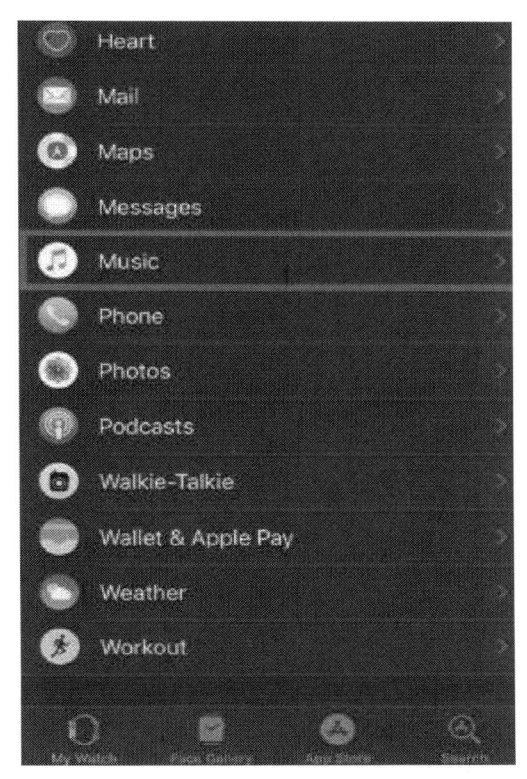

Add Playlists and Albums to Apple Watch

Here is how to add albums and playlists from your iPhone to your Apple Watch:

- Launch the Apple Watch app on your iPhone
- Click on **My Watch,** then click on **Music.**
- Scroll to **Playlists & Albums,** then click on **Add Music.**

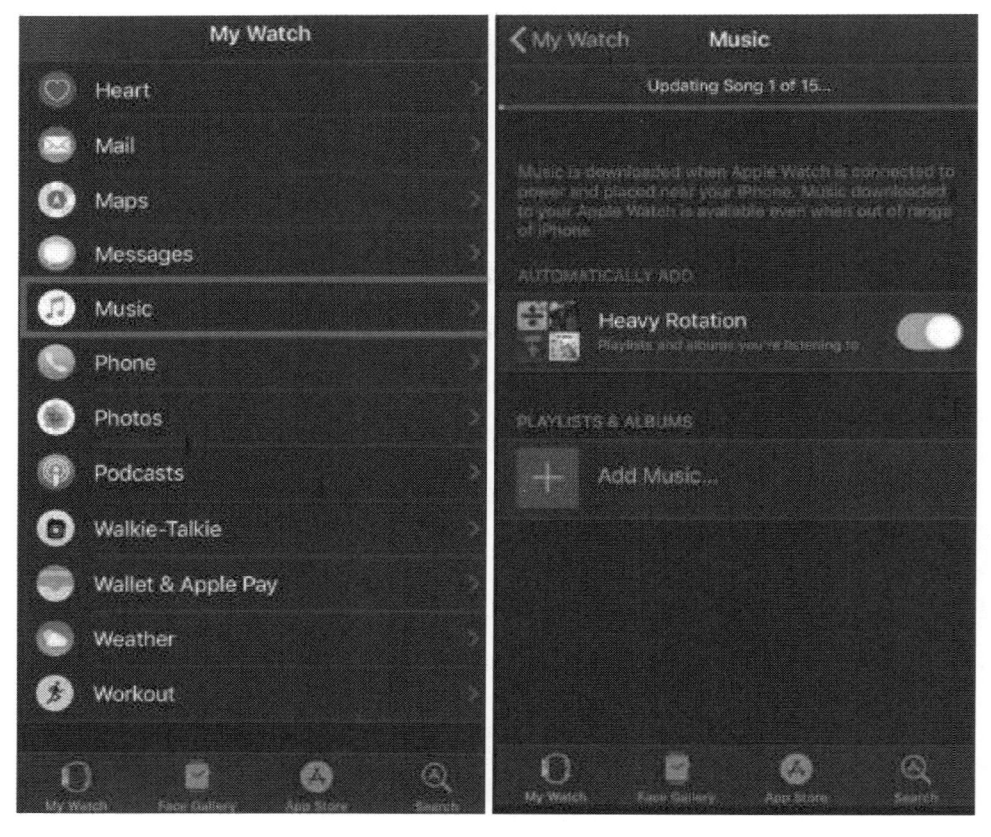

- Choose the playlists and albums that you want to add to your Apple Watch.

Add a Workout Playlist

Workout playlists that you add will automatically begin to play whenever you start a workout except if you have another audio playing before you begin the workout. Here is how to add the workout playlist:

- Launch the Apple Watch app on your iPhone
- Click on **My Watch,** then click on **Workout.**
- Click on **Workout Playlist,** then select a playlist.

Sync Music to Your Apple Watch

Follow the steps below to sync music to your Apple Watch.

- Connect your Apple Watch to its charger and ensure that it is charging. Then place your iPhone close to your watch.
- Open the **Settings** app on your iPhone. Then click on **Bluetooth.** Check that Bluetooth is enabled.

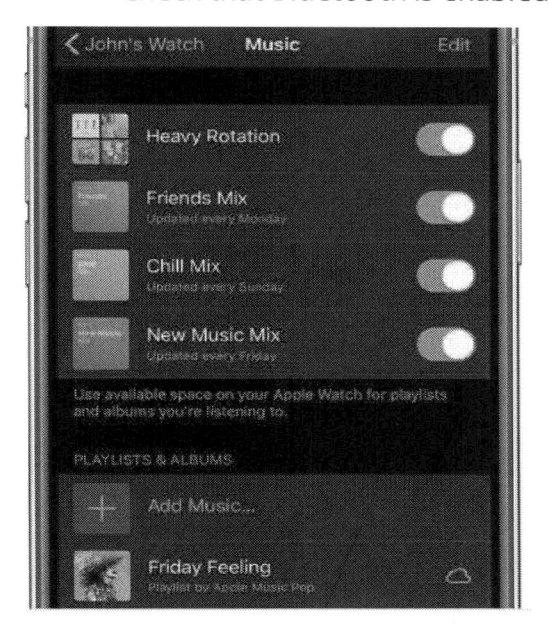

- Launch the Apple Watch app on your iPhone. Then click on **My Watch.** Click on **Music,** then click on **Add Music.**
- Click on the button beside the music that you want to add.

See How Much Music You Have on Your Watch

There are two ways to view the amount of music stored on your watch:

On Apple Watch

- Click on the Settings app on your watch's home screen.
- Click on **General.**
- Then click on **Usage.**

On iPhone

- Launch the Apple Watch app on your iPhone
- Click on **My Watch.**
- Click on **General.**
- Then click on **Usage.**

Remove Music From Apple Watch

Music deleted from the Apple Watch is not also deleted from your phone. Follow the steps below to delete music from your watch.

- Launch the Apple Watch app on your iPhone
- Click on **My Watch.** Click on **Music.**
- Disable the automatically added playlists that you no longer want on your watch.
- To remove the music that you added manually, click on **Edit,** then tap the icon beside the music you no longer want.

- Then click on **Delete.**

Listen to Music from Music Library

You can use your Apple Watch to listen to albums and playlists that you created on your iPhone. You can also listen to any music from Apple Music or on audio apps like iHeartRadio, Pandora, and Spotify.

- Set up your headphones, speaker, or earbuds via Bluetooth on the watch.

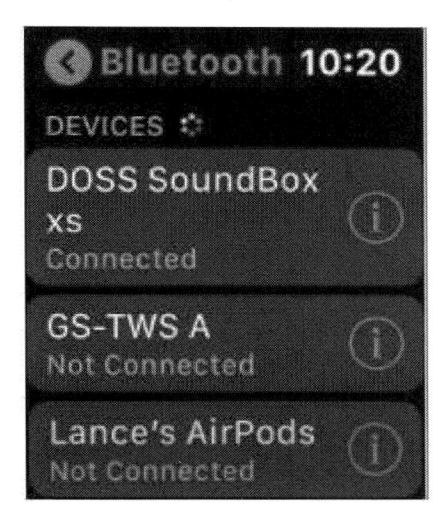

- Launch the Apple Music app on your watch's home screen.
- Turn the Digital Crown to swipe through your albums for songs stored on your watch. Click on an album or a playlist to play it.
- From the player, you may choose to skip to the next song, go back, pause, resume, or control the volume.

Play Music From iPhone

Follow the steps below to play music on your Apple Watch from your iPhone. You do not require Bluetooth pairing for this to work.

- Open the Music app on your watch's home screen and scroll to the top of your screen.
- Tap **On iPhone,** then click on an album, playlist, song, or artist to play it.

Listen to Apple Music

If you are a subscriber to Apple Music, you can listen to songs from the Apple Music catalog or ask Siri to play songs for you. The app also suggests music based on your likes and the music you listened to in the past. Follow the steps below to play music chosen for you.

- From the home screen of the watch, open the Music app and scroll to the top of your screen.
- Click on **For You** to see all the playlists and albums based on your likes.
- Click on an album, category, or playlist, then click on the Play button to listen.

Follow the steps below to ask Siri to play songs for you.

- Raise your wrist, then ask Siri for a song, artist, genre, or album.

Open the Up Next Queue

While one song is playing, other songs are lined up in the **Up Next** queue. Here is how to access this list:

- Open the Music app on your watch.
- While an album or playlist is playing, click on .
- Click on any song in the queue to play it.
- To add more music to the queue, swipe to the left side of the song you want to add, then tap the button. Click on **Play Next** or **Play Later.** If you selected **Play Later,** the music would be added to the end of the queue.

Chapter 6: Podcasts and AudioBooks

Sync Podcasts to Your Apple Watch

By default, charging your watch will automatically sync all the podcasts that you subscribe to. However, here is a manual way to sync your podcasts:

- Open the **Settings** app on your iPhone. Then click on **Podcasts** and ensure that **Sync Podcast** is enabled.
- Launch the Apple Watch app on your iPhone. Then click on **My Watch.** Click on **Podcasts.**
- Scroll to **Add Episodes From** and click on **Custom** and toggle on the shows that you want.

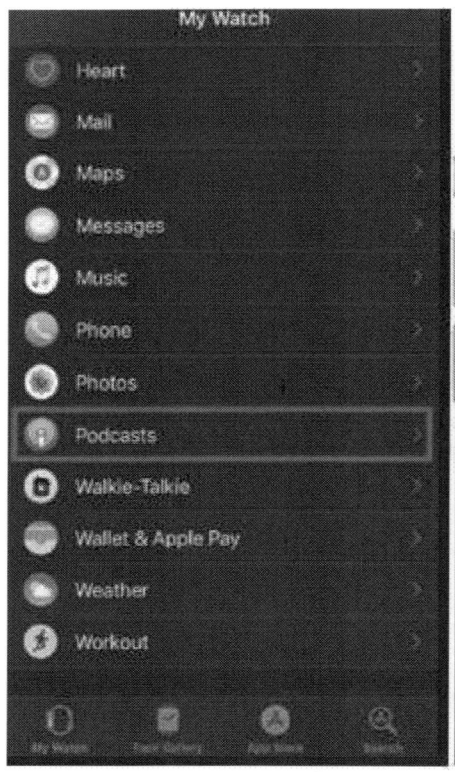

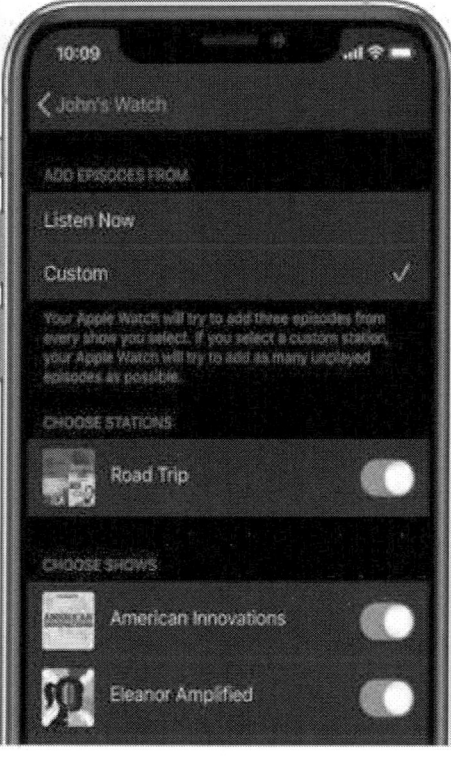

- Launch the Podcasts app on your iPhone, search for the show, then click on **Subscribe.**
- Once you listen to an episode, it becomes automatically removed from your watch.

Sync Audiobooks

Follow the steps below to sync audiobooks to your watch:

- Connect your Apple Watch to its charger and ensure that it is charging. Then place your iPhone close to your watch.
- Open the **Settings** app on your iPhone. Then click on **Bluetooth.** Check that Bluetooth is enabled.
- Launch the Apple Watch app on your iPhone. Then click on **My Watch.**
- Click on **Audiobooks,** then click on **Add Audiobooks** to add a new audiobook.
- Audiobooks with the ☁ button are waiting to be synced, while audiobooks without the ☁ button are already synced to your watch.

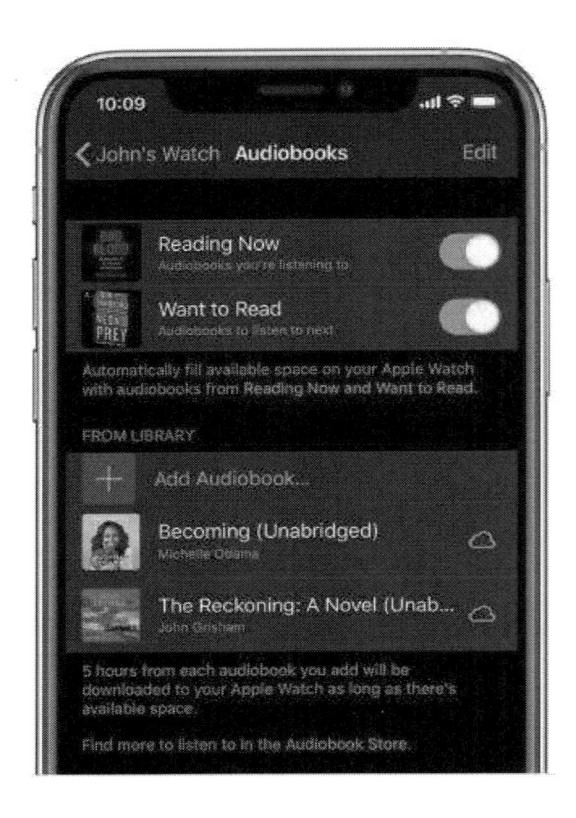

Add a Workout Podcasts

Workout podcasts that you add will automatically begin to play whenever you start a workout except if another music or audio is playing. Here is how to create a workout playlist:
- Launch the Apple Watch app on your iPhone
- Click on **My Watch,** then click on **Workout.**
- Click on **Workout Playlist,** then select a playlist.

If you do not want the playlist to begin playing when you start a workout, follow the steps below to disable the **Now Playing** option:
- Launch the Apple Watch app on your iPhone

- Click on **My Watch,** then click on **General.**
- Click on **Wake Screen,** then disable **Auto-Launch Audio Apps.**

Listen to Podcasts Stored on the Watch

- Set up your headphones, speaker, or earbuds via Bluetooth.

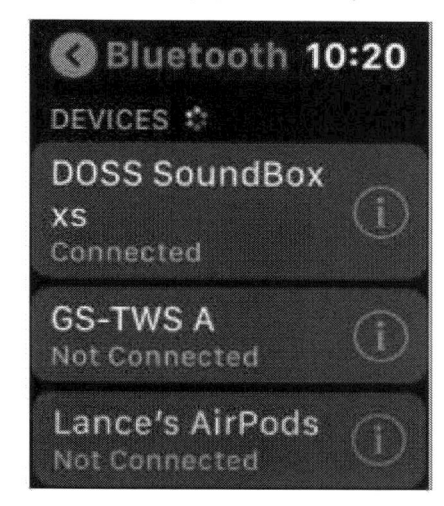

- Launch the Podcast app on your watch's home screen.
- Turn the Digital Crown to swipe through your subscribed podcasts. Click on a podcast to play it.

Play Podcasts from iPhone

Follow the steps below to play Podcasts from your iPhone to your Apple Watch. You do not require Bluetooth pairing for this to work.

- Open the Podcasts app on your watch and scroll to the top of your screen.
- Tap **On iPhone,** then click on your preferred options: **Stations, Episodes, Listen Now,** or **Shows.**
- Click on an episode to play it.

Play Podcast from Your Library

Place your iPhone close to your Apple Watch to listen to podcasts from your podcast library.

- Open the Podcasts app on your watch.
- Click on **Library.**
- Then click on your preferred options: **Stations, Episodes, Listen Now,** or **Shows.**
- Click on an episode to play it.

Play Podcasts with Siri

To ask Siri to play a podcast for you

- Raise your wrist, then tell Siri to play a show.

Chapter 7: The Workouts App

The Apple Watch has a built-in workout app that you can use to track your progress at different health activities like jogging, swimming, walking, biking, and so on. With the app, you can select a specific distance, time, or the number of calories you want to burn. You can also choose to record a free-flowing workout with defined restrictions. As you proceed on the activity, you will view the calories burned, time spent, your heart rate as well as the distance you have traveled. Go to the Activity app on your iPhone to view your workout history. You can also view your latest stat right on the Apple Watch.

Start a Workout

Follow the steps below to begin a workout:

- Launch the Workout app on your Watch's home screen.
- Turn the Digital Crown to swipe through the different workouts until you find the one you want. Click on the exercise that you want, or click on **Add Workout** at the end of your screen if the exercise you want is not included on the screen.

- To create a goal, tap the **More** icon beside the workout type, then choose the option that applies: either **Open, Calorie, Distance,** or **Time.** Click on + / − or turn the Digital Crown to set your goals.
- Click **Start** to begin.

Note: to begin a workout without creating a goal, simply click on the workout type.

Pause Workout

To pause your workout,

- Tap on your watch screen to wake your watch and display the Workout app.
- Swipe right on the app to go to the workout app menu.
- Click on the Pause button to pause the workout.

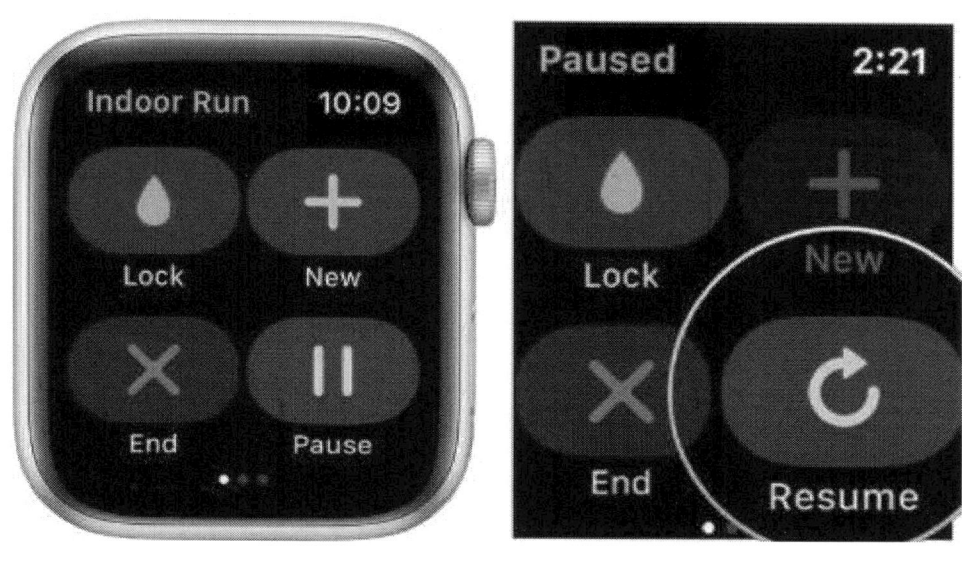

- Alternatively, press the side button and the Digital Crown at the same time to pause. Press both buttons again to resume.

End Workout

At the end of your workout, you need to let the Apple Watch know that you are done with the workout so that it can record your progress.

- Tap on your watch screen to wake your watch and display the Workout app.
- Swipe right on the app to go to the workout app menu.
- Click on the End button ⊗ to end the workout.
- Then tap **Done** to confirm your action.

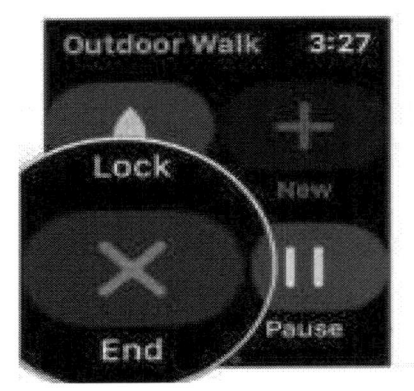

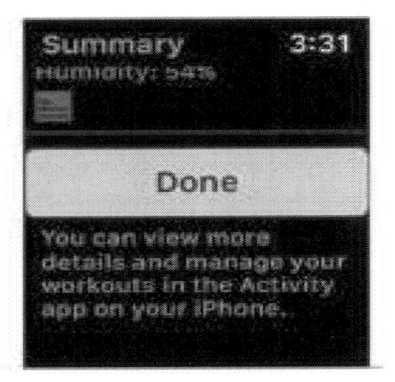

Lock Workout

You may lock your watch screen during a workout to prevent accidental taps. Here is how to:

- Swipe right on the workout app to display the menu screen.
- Then click on the Lock button 🔵.
- Turn the digital crown to unlock your screen.

Track Your Progress

To see your progress during a workout,

- Raise your wrist.
- Then turn the digital crown to display the metric that you wish to see.

Note: when cycling, your Apple Watch taps you at every five kilometers or miles while for walking or running, the watch taps you at every kilometer or mile.

Set Target Pace for Outdoor Runs

When you set a target pace for an outdoor run, your watch will vibrate on your wrist to update you if you are behind or ahead of your set pace once you cross a mile. Here is how to set the target pace:

- Launch the Workout app on your Watch.
- Turn the Digital Crown to swipe through the different workouts until you get to **Outdoor Run** or **Indoor Run.** Tap the More icon beside **Outdoor Run** or **Indoor Run.**
- Click on **Set Alert,** then click on **Ok.**
- Set your target time, then click on **Done.**
- Select either **Rolling** or **Average**, then tap <.

- ✓ Choose **Rolling** if you want your one-mile pace taken at the moment or **Average** for your average pace for all the distance you covered.
- Tap **Start** to begin your workout. Tap the screen to skip the three seconds countdown.

Follow the steps below to change the target pace

- Click on **Outdoor Run** in the Workout app.
- Then tap the More icon .
- Click on the pace alert at the end of your screen, then click on the current pace to modify it.

Combine Multiple Activities in a Single Workout

You can choose to have more than one workout activity per time. here is how to

- Launch the workout app and start your first workout.

- Swipe right on the app and tap the plus icon ✚ , then turn the digital crown to select the next activity.
- When you are done with all the activities, swipe right on your screen, then click on **End**.
- Use the Digital crown to navigate through the summary of the results.
- Then tap **Done** at the bottom of your screen to save the activity.

Tip: you do not need your iPhone to go on an outdoor workout as the watch has a built-in GPS that gives accurate distance measurement.

Change Workout Metrics

You can modify the default metrics that display during a workout. Here is how to do this

- Open the Apple Watch app on your iPhone.
- Click on **My Watch** at the bottom of your screen.
- Then click on **Workout** and select **Workout View.**
- Choose either **Single Metric** or **Multiple Metric.**
- For Single Metric, use the Digital Crown to swipe through all the metrics while exercising.
- If you chose Multiple metrics, you could select up to five metrics for each workout. Click on a workout type on your screen, and click on **Edit.** Then tap the ⊖ button to delete or the green button to add

metrics, or tap and hold the ≡ icon to modify the order of the metric.

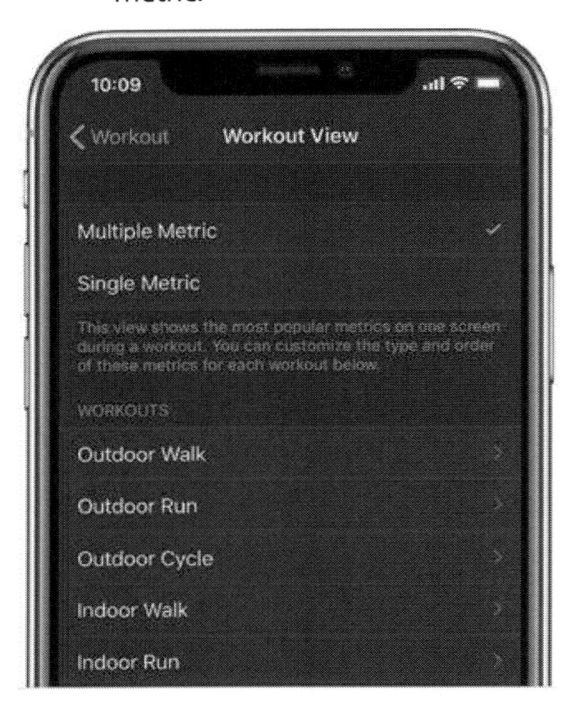

Add a Workout

You can add new workout types to the workout app on your Apple Watch.

- Open the Workout app 🏃 on your Apple watch.
- Scroll down to the end of your screen and click on **Add Workout.**
- Then scroll down on your screen until you find and select the new workout.
- If the workout type you desire is not on the list, click on **other.**

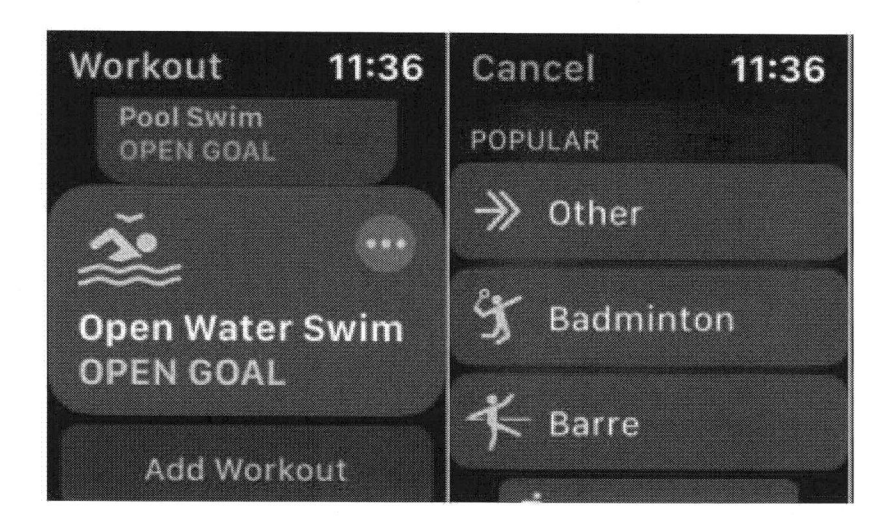

Listen to Music During a Workout

To listen to music while working out,

- Swipe left on the workout app to go to the **Now Playing** screen.
- Now select your music and use the Bluetooth headphones to control the volume.

Reminder to Start a Workout

Whenever your Apple Watch detects that you are working out or performing some type of physical activity, it will tap you on the wrist to confirm and prompt you to record the workout session on your watch. You can click on an option within the notification to change the workout type, record the workout, or dismiss the notification.

This feature is enabled by default, but you can disable it and turn it on later in the future. Here is how to:

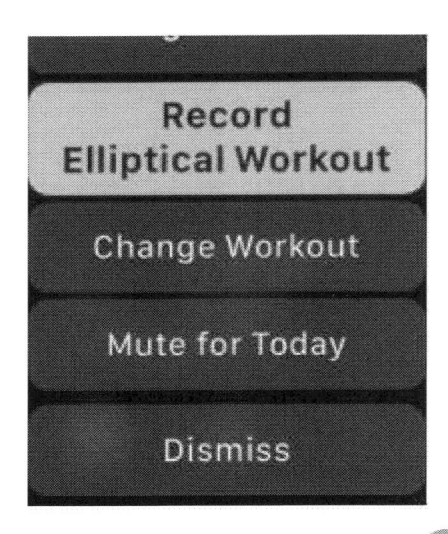

- Open the Settings app on your watch.
- Scroll down and click on **Workout.**
- Then toggle on **Start Workout Reminder.**

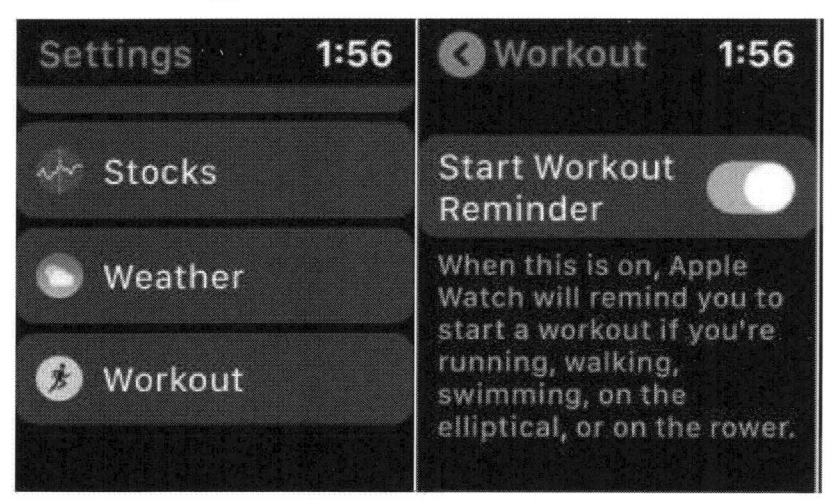

Get Reminders to End Your Workout

Your watch can also tell when you are no longer performing a physical exercise. Your watch will tap you on the wrist to confirm. You can click on an option within the notification to dismiss the notification and continue your workout, or pause/ end the workout. If you do not respond to the notification, the watch will continue to record the workout until you manually pause or end it. Here is how to set this reminder.

- Open the Settings app on your watch.
- Scroll down and click on **Workout.**
- Then toggle on **End Workout Reminder.**

Save Power During Workouts

The Power Saving mode on your Watch will help to preserve battery life by disabling the heart rate sensor, Always-On display, as well as cellular data. Your watch will continue to calculate the distance covered, active calories, elapsed time, and pace. Follow the guide below to enable **Power Saving mode**.

- Open the **Watch** app on your iPhone.
- Click on **My Watch** at the bottom of your screen, then select **Workout.**

- Now enable or disable **Power Saving Mode.**

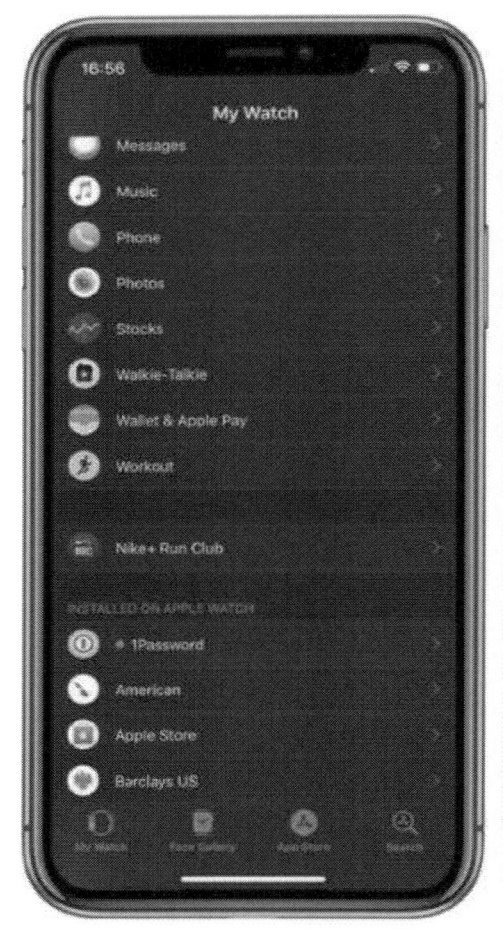

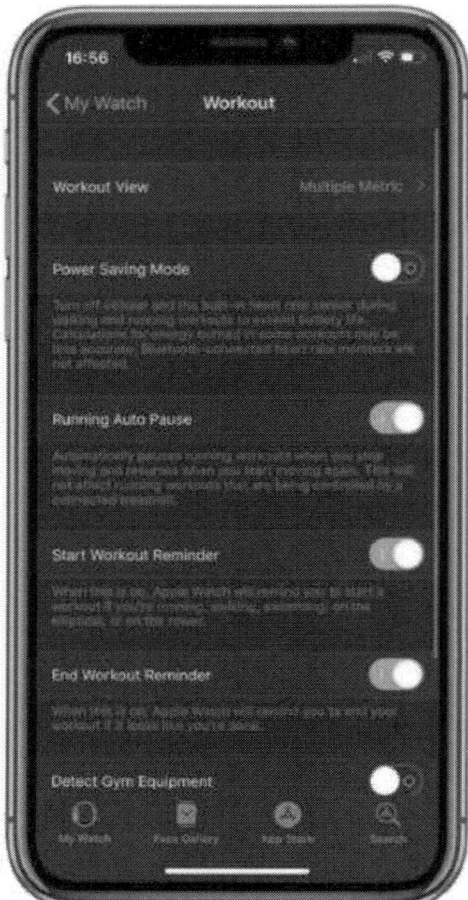

You can also control this on the Apple Watch itself

- Open the Settings app on your watch.
- Scroll down and click on **Workout.**
- Then toggle on **Power Saving Mode.**

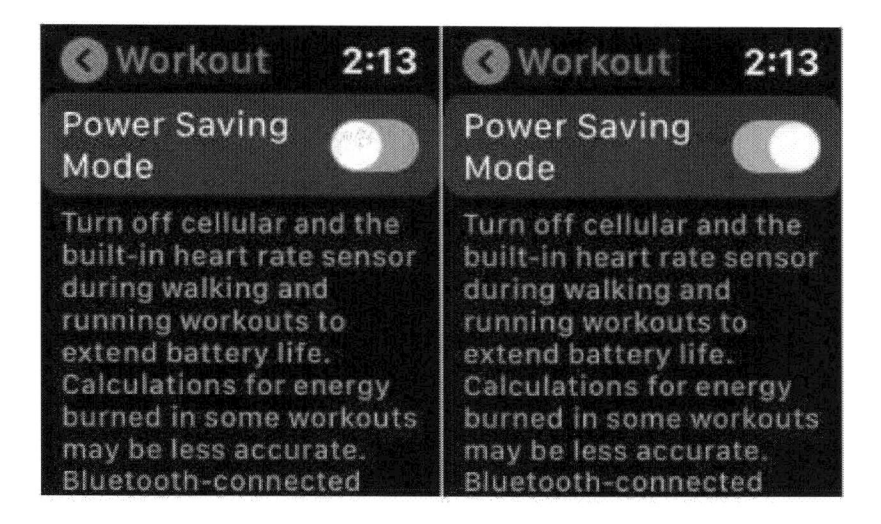

Enable Running Auto Pause

Enable this feature if you want your watch to automatically pause your runs when you cease to move and to resume the moment you start moving again.

- Open the Settings app on your watch.
- Scroll down and click on **Workout.**
- Then toggle on **Running Auto Pause.**
- You may also toggle on **Detect Gym Equipment** if you want to synchronize your workouts with gym equipment.

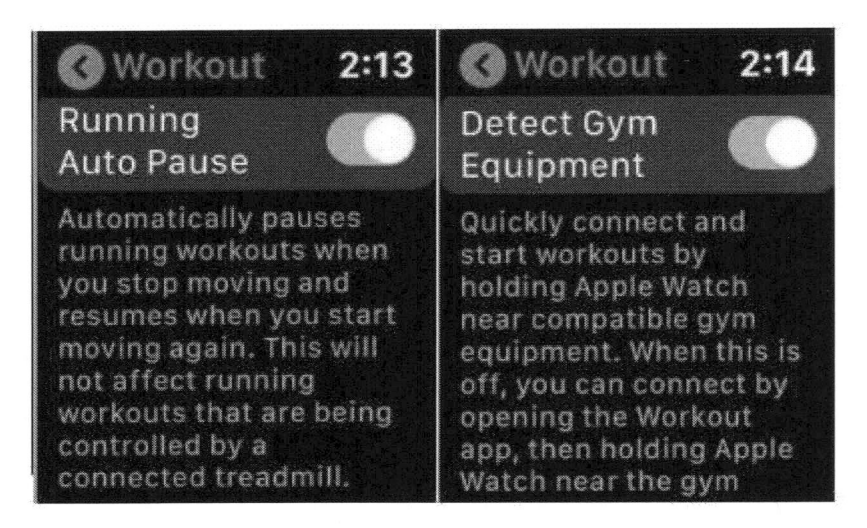

To configure this setting on your iPhone, follow the steps below:

- Open the Apple Watch app on your iPhone and click on **My Watch.**
- Click on **Workout,** then toggle on **Running Auto Pause.**

If you prefer to pause your runs manually,

- Press the side button and the digital crown at the same time to pause. Press the two buttons again to resume your run.

View Workout Activity

You can view your workout history on your Apple Watch via the Activity app. The Activity app will display your activity for the same day in circle-like icons . The red circle shows the amount of calories you burned since the beginning of the day, the green color shows the time spent so far on physical activities, while the blue shows the number of hours you have been standing. It is expected that you will close the ring for each of the categories. Press hard on the circle to change your move goal or access a weekly summary.

- Click on the weekly summary to view a graph for the week showing your total number of steps, distances, calories, and every other goal you achieved.

- Click on **Change Move Goal** to reduce or increase your daily calorie target.

- Tap **Done** to save.

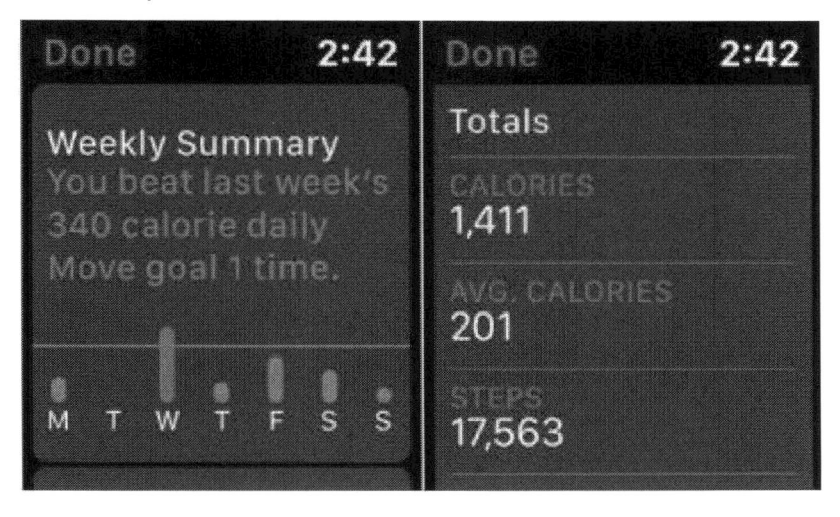

View Your Activity History

For more detailed information on your workout history, go to the Activity app on your iPhone. On this app, you will view details like your activity history, workout history, and your awards.

- Open the Activity app on your iPhone.
- Click on the **History** tab to see your activity details and data for the present day. Click on the left arrow beside the month at the top of your screen to show a calendar. Choose a defined date to view specific information.

View Workout History

Go to the Workout tab to view your workout activity for the month.

- Open the Activity app on your iPhone.
- Click on the **Workout** tab.
- Click on the year at the top of your screen to view your workout history month by month. Click on one month to view more details for that month.
- Click on the **All Workouts** link at the top of your screen and filter the list to show just what you want to view.

View Activity Trends

The **Trend** tab in the Activity app shows your daily activity and workout trend, including details on how much distance you travel, how long you stand, how long you exercise, and how many calories you burn. You will also receive advice on how to achieve better results for your specified goal.

- Open the Activity app on your iPhone.
- Click on the **Trend** tab, then click on any desired item for more details.

Share Activity Data

The Apple Watch allows you to challenge another user to a competition. But you need first to share your activity data with the user. To do this

- Open the Activity app on your iPhone and click on the **Sharing** tab at the bottom of your screen.
- Then click on **Get Started.**

- Click the ╋button, then choose the receiver(s) from your contact list. Then tap **Send**.
- The receiver will need to open the Activity app and click on **Accept** to accept the invitation, after which the name of the receiver will appear on your sharing screen.

Follow the steps below to invite a friend directly on the Apple Watch
- Launch the Activity app on your watch.
- Swipe till you get to the Sharing screen.
- Click on **Invite A Friend** at the bottom of your screen.

Start a Competition on iPhone

After you have successfully shared your activity data with a contact, follow the steps below to invite the person to a workout challenge.

- Click on the **Sharing** tab on the Activity app on your iPhone.
- Click on the name of the contact.
- Then click on **Compete with (Name)**.
- Then tap **Invite (Name)**
- Select the competition type.
- Once the contact responds in his or her own Activity app, the competition will begin.

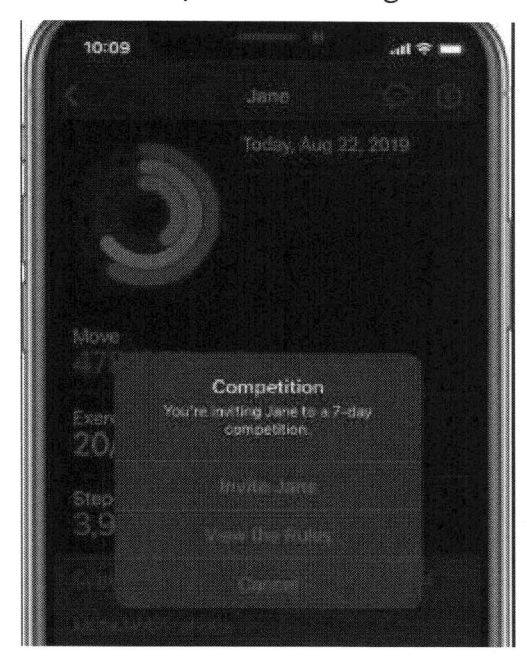

Start a Competition on Apple Watch

To invite a friend on the Apple Watch, follow the steps below

- Launch the Activity app on your watch.

- Swipe till you get to the Sharing screen, then click on a friend.
- Click on **Compete** at the bottom of your screen.
- Then tap **Invite (Name)**
- Select the competition type.
- Once the contact responds in his or her own Activity app, the competition will begin.

Compare Activity Data on Apple Watch

After your friend must have accepted the challenge, you can view and compare the progress of yourself and your friend with the steps below:

- Launch the Activity app on your watch.
- Swipe left to see the stats for all the participants.
- Click on a name to explode and view more details.

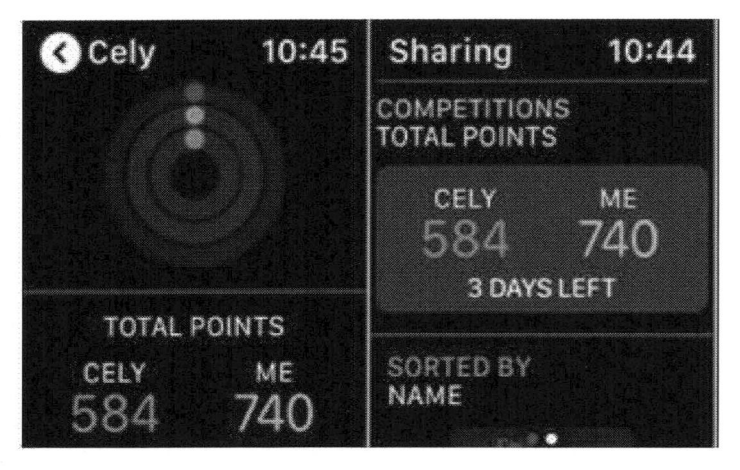

Compare Activity Data on iPhone

To check the progress on your phone,

- Open the Activity app and click on the **Sharing** tab.
- The next screen will show the progress for each participant. Click on a name to view more details.

Complete a Challenge

At the end of the challenge, you will get a prompt from your watch, notifying you that the challenge has ended. The Activity app will show the winner of the challenge as well as the final numbers. You may then choose to invite the person to another challenge, send them a message, or dismiss the screen.

Hide Your Progress

You may decide to stop sharing your activity data with a friend. However, this option will not apply to persons that you are competing with.

- Click on the **Sharing** tab on the Activity app on your iPhone.
- Click on the friend that you wish to hide your activity from.
- Then click on **Hide My Activity.** This way, your friend will be unable to see your activity. Note that you can still view the other party's activity until they hide their progress from you.
- Click on **Show My Activity** to begin sharing again.

Remove a Friend

This is another way to stop sharing your progress with a friend.

- Click on the **Sharing** tab on the Activity app on your iPhone.
- Click on the friend that you wish to hide your activity from.
- Then tap **Remove Friend.** Neither of you will be able to view each other's activity.
- You will need to send a new invite to begin sharing again.

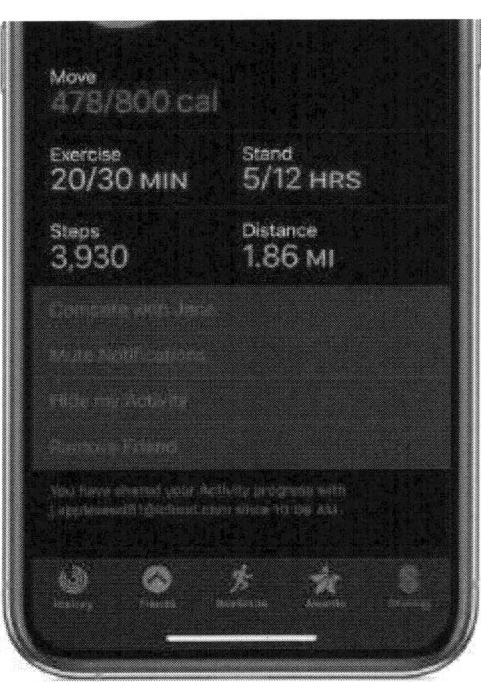

Chapter 8: The Breathe App

The breath app helps you to relax and focus on your breathing. The app takes you through several deep breaths as well as sends you reminders to breathe.

Start a Breathe Session

- Launch the Breathe app on your watch.
- Click on **Start,** then slowly inhale as the animation enlarges, then exhale as the animation shrinks.

Customize Breathing Reminders

Your watch reminds you to breathe throughout the day. Here is how to disable or modify these reminders.

- Launch the Watch app on your phone, click on the **My Watch** tab, then click on **Breathe.**
- Click on either **Send to Notification Centre, Allow Notifications, or Notifications Off** to set your notification preference.
- Click on **Breathe Reminders** to customize the frequency at which you get the reminders.

Set Duration of a Breathe Session.

- Launch the Breathe app on your watch and use the digital crown to increase the duration.
- Tap **Start** to begin.

- To use the set duration as your default, launch the Watch app on your phone, click on the **My Watch** tab, then toggle on **Use Previous Duration.**

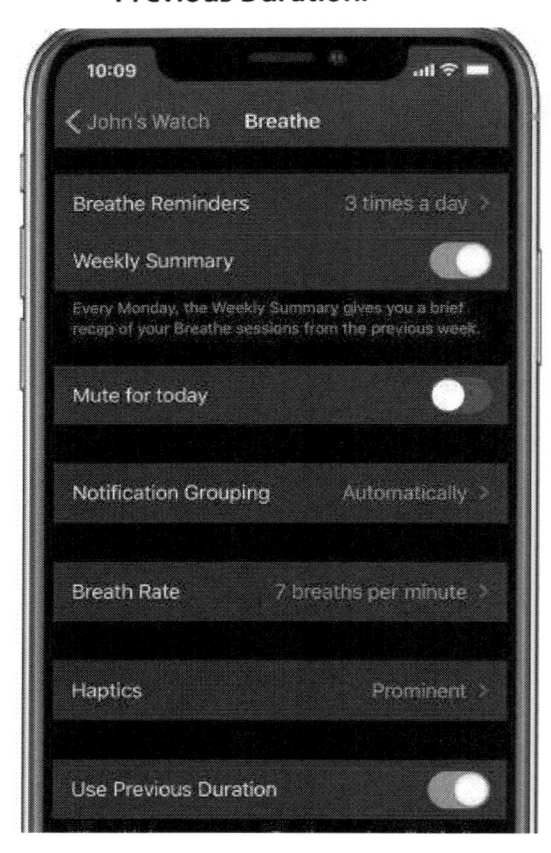

View Heart Rate During Breathe Sessions

- Launch the Health app on your phone and click on the **Browse** tab.
- Click on **Heart,** then click on **Heart Rate.**
- Click on **Show All Filters,** then move up and click on **Breathe.**

Chapter 9: Heart Rate on Apple Watch

Knowing your heart rate tells you how your body is performing. With your Apple Watch, you can check your heart rate while working out or take a new reading whenever you wish.

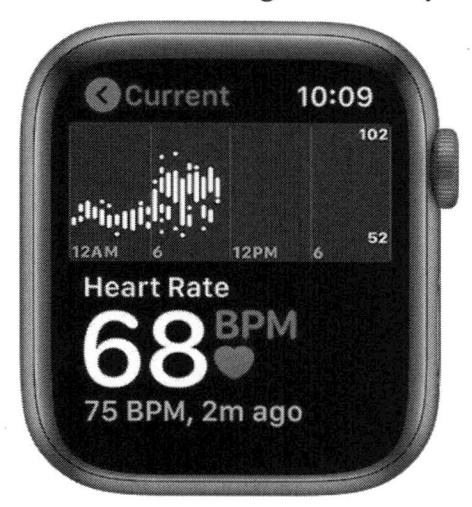

Monitor Your Heart Rate

The watch has a built-in Heart rate app that you can use to view your heart rate at any time. As long as you wear your watch, the device will continue to check your heart rate. Here is how to view your heart rate:

- Open the Heart rate app on your watch.
- Glance at your watch face to allow the watch measure and show you your current heart rate.

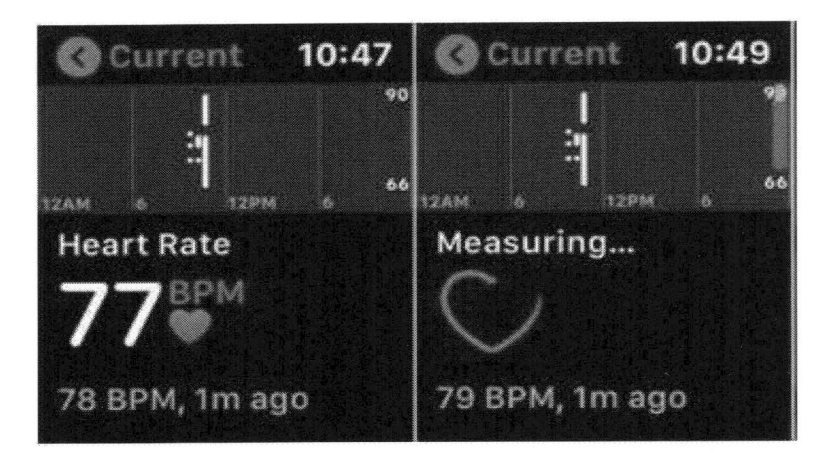

- Click on the arrow at the top left side of your screen to view your resting rate, current heart rate, and your average rate.

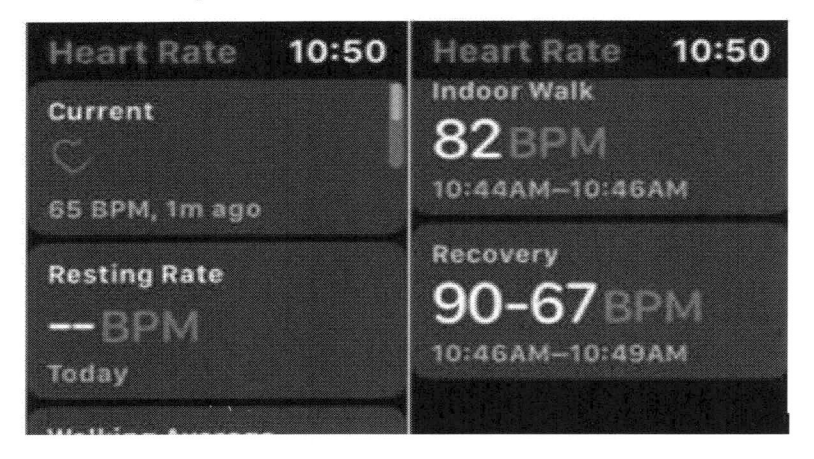

Check Your Heart Rate During a Workout

The watch automatically shows your current heart rate on the Multiple Metric workout view. Follow the steps below to customize the metrics that should have the current heart rate.

- Open the Apple Watch app on your iPhone.
- Click on **My Watch** at the bottom of your screen.
- Then click on **Workout** and select **Workout View.**

- Choose either **Single Metric** or **Multiple Metric.**

View A Graph of Your Heart Rate Data

To view details of your heart rate over a certain period, follow the steps below:

- Launch the Health app on your phone.
- Scroll to the bottom right side of your screen and click on **Browse.**
- Click on **Heart,** then click on **Heart Rate.**
- To include Heart Rate in the summary, swipe up on your screen and click on **Add to Favorites.**
- Click on **Show All Filters** to view the range of your heart rate within a selected period.

Enable Heart Rate Data

This feature is turned on by default. Follow the steps below to disable or enable it if turned off.

- Open the Apple Watch app on your iPhone.
- Click on **My Watch** at the bottom of your screen.
- Then click on **Privacy** and toggle off/ on **Heart Rate.**

Enable High or Low Heart Rate Notification

Turn on heart rate notification to receive a prompt when your heart rate remains above or below a specified threshold after you stay inactive for a minimum of ten minutes.

- Open the Apple Watch app on your iPhone.
- Click on **My Watch** at the bottom of your screen.

- Click on **Heart,** then click on **High Heart Rate** and choose your desired heart rate.
- Return to the previous screen, click on **Low Heart Rate** and choose your desired heart rate.

Set Up Irregular Heart Rhythm Notification

Set up this notification to receive a prompt whenever your watch notices an irregular heart rhythm that may be atrial fibrillation (AFib).

- Open the Apple Watch app on your iPhone.
- Click on **My Watch** at the bottom of your screen.
- Click on **Heart,** then toggle on **Irregular Rhythm,** under **Heart Rate Notification.**

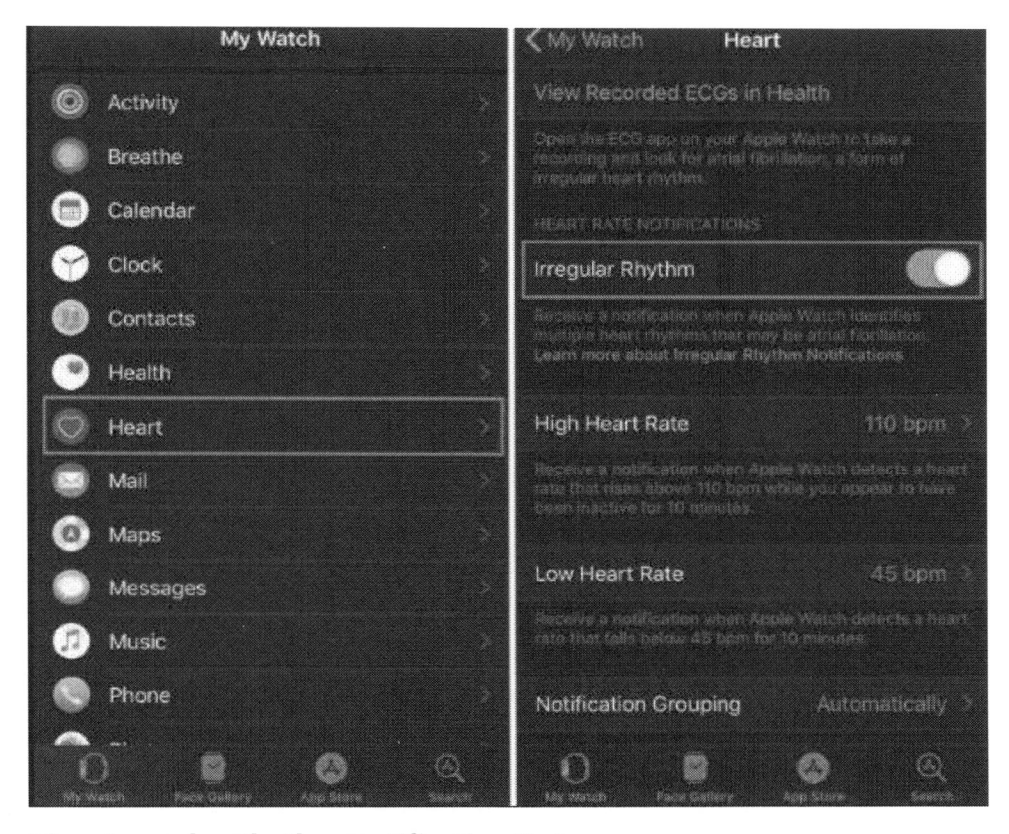

View Irregular Rhythm Notification Data

To view details of the irregular rhythm notification,

- Open the Health app on your iPhone.
- Click on the **Browse** tab at the bottom of your screen.
- Then click on **Heart.**
- Click on **Irregular Rhythm Notifications** at the bottom of your screen.
- Click on **Show All Data** to view all the details collected.

- Toggle on **Add to Favorites** if you want the Irregular Rhythm Notification widget to be displayed on the Heart screen under **Health Data.**

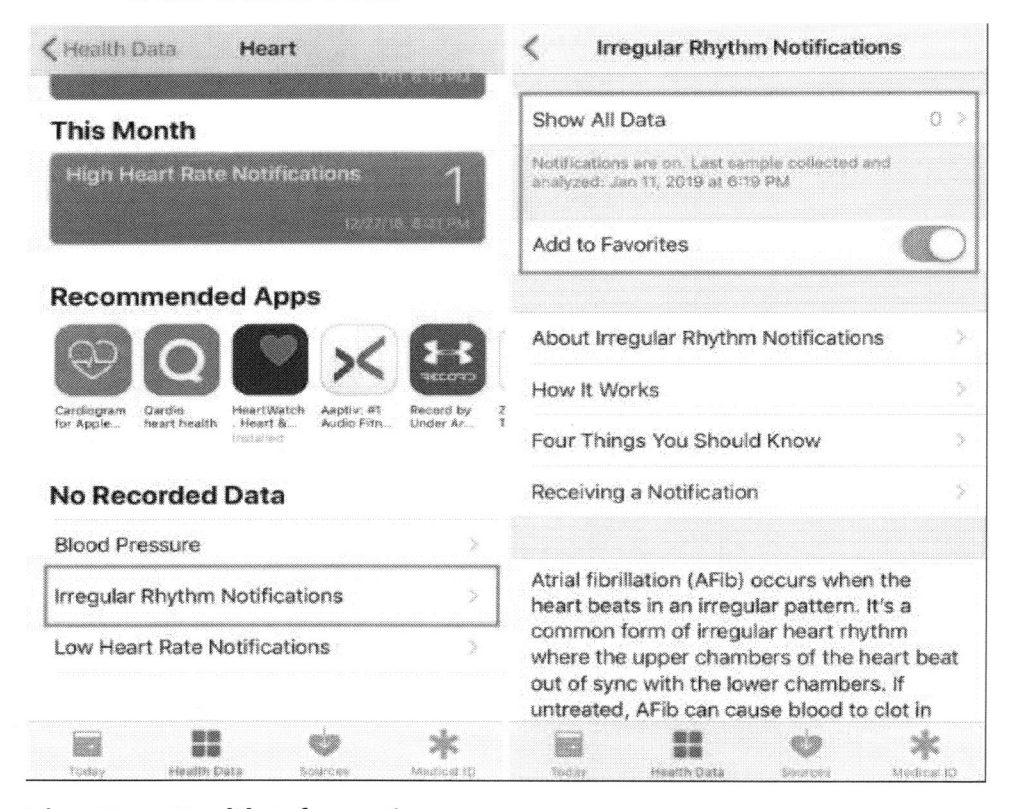

View Your Health Information

The Health app on the iPhone allows you to record your health information and view same on your watch. Here is how to set this up:

- Open the Health app on your iPhone and click on your profile picture at the top right side of your screen.
- Click on **Health Profile** to record your data like blood type, gender, and so on.

- Return to the previous screen and click on **Medical ID** to enter details like your health condition, medical history, and medications.

After you have inputted your health details on the Health app, follow the steps below to view this information on the Apple Watch:

- Open the Settings app on your watch and click on **Health.**
- Click on each entry to view the registered details.

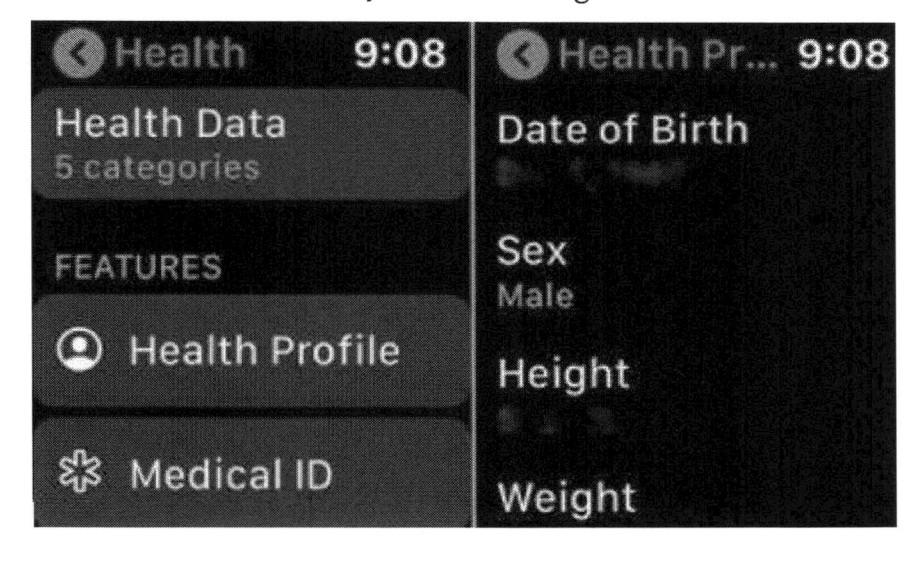

Chapter 10: ECG on Apple Watch

The ECG app on the Apple Watch records your heart rhythm and heartbeat using the electrical heart sensor. The app then records an electrocardiogram, which shows the electrical pulses that your heartbeat is made of. The app uses these pulses to determine your heart rate as well as tell if the lower and upper chambers of the heart are in rhythm. When the two upper chambers of the heart experience chaotic electric signals, it can lead to an irregular and often rapid heart rate known as Atrial fibrillation (Afib). This condition can cause blood clots within the upper chambers of your heart and may spread to other organs, leading to blocked blood flow.

Set Up the ECG App

Ensure that the iOS on your iPhone is updated to the current version then follow the steps below:

- Open the Apple Watch app on your iPhone.
- Click on **My Watch** at the bottom of your screen.
- Click on **Heart,** then click on **Set Up the ECG App in Health,** then follow the instructions on your screen to complete the setup.

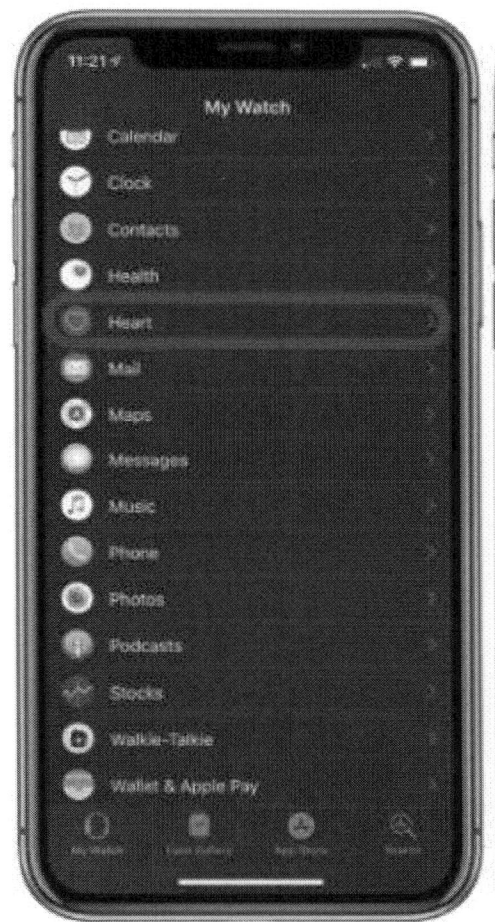

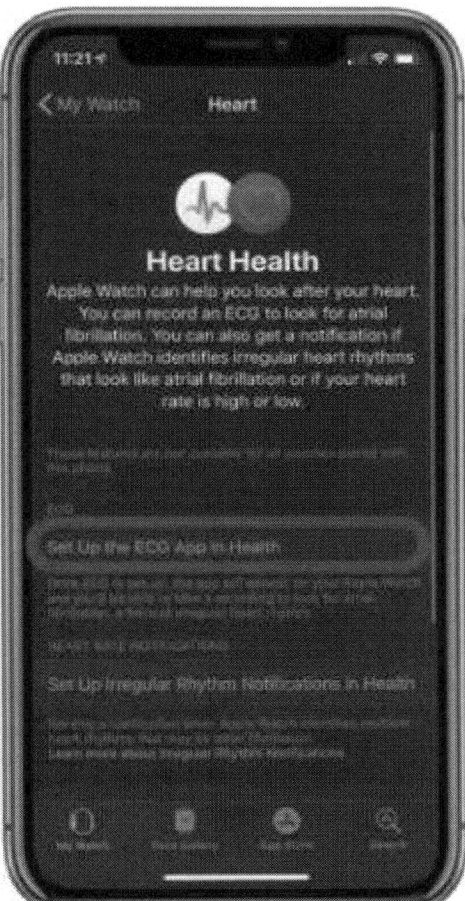

Here is a more direct way to set up the ECG app:
- Open the Health app on your iPhone.
- Click on the **Browse** tab at the bottom of your screen.
- Then click on **Heart.**
- Swipe down and click on **Electrocardiogram (ECG).**
- Then click on **Set Up ECG** and follow the prompts to complete the setup.

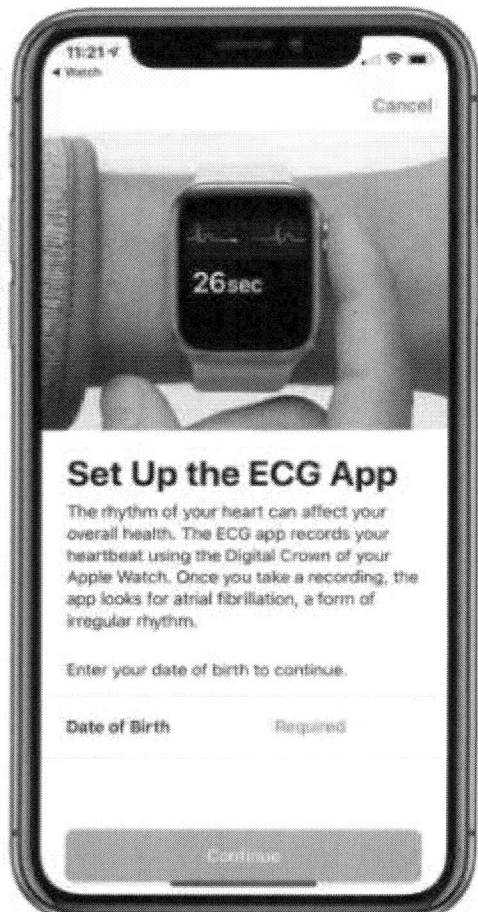

Take an ECG

The best time to take an ECG is when you have symptoms like skipped or rapid heartbeat or other health concerns or even when you receive an irregular rhythm notification. Here is how to take an ECG:

- Check that your watch is snug and placed on the wrist that you selected in the Apple Watch app. To confirm the wrist, launch the Apple Watch app on your iPhone, click on the **My watch** tap, click on **General,** then click on **Watch orientation.**

- Push the Digital Crown to go to the home screen, then tap the ECG app to open it.
- Place your arm on your lap or a table.
- Using the hand opposite the watch, place your finger on the Digital Crown for thirty seconds to measure the electrical signals of your heart.
- When the recording is complete, the app will display your heart rate and sinus rhythm.
- Click on **Done** if the reading goes well or click on **Add Symptoms** to record any symptom you feel.
- Then click on **Save** and click on **Done** to complete.

View and Share ECG Data on the Health App

To view or share your ECG reading, follow the steps below
- Launch the Health app on your phone.
- Navigate to the **Browse** tab, then click on **Heart.**
- Click on **Electrocardiogram (ECG).**
- Click on the ECG result you wish to share with your doctor.
- Then click on **Export a PDF for Your Doctor.**
- Click on the Share button at the top of your screen to share or print the PDF.
- Choose how you want to share the report.

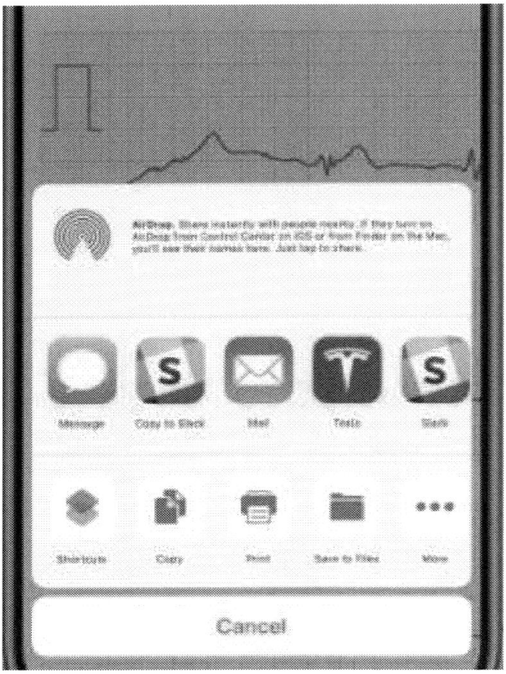
Cancel

Chapter 11: Fall Detection

The Apple Watch has a built-in feature known as Fall Detection that allows your watch to tell when you have a hard fall; the watch will vibrate on your wrist and also sound an alarm. With the alarm comes the prompt to either contact local emergency services or dismiss the alert. To dismiss the alert, simply tap **I'm OK** on your screen or press the digital crown of your watch and tap **Close** in the top left side of your screen.

If the watch detects a movement, it allows you to respond to the alert before it calls for emergency services, if needed. However, if you remain immobile for one minute, the watch will automatically call for emergency service. At the end of the call, the watch will send a message to your emergency contacts, providing them with your location and informing them that you had a hard fall, and a call has 3w2wq been placed to emergency services.

Enable or Disable Fall Detection

This feature is enabled automatically for persons age 55 and above if you inputted your age when setting up your watch or in the Health app.

However, you may follow the steps below to enable or disable this feature

- Launch the Apple Watch app on your phone and navigate to the **My Watch** tab.
- Click on **Emergency SOS.**
- Then toggle on or off **Fall Detection.**

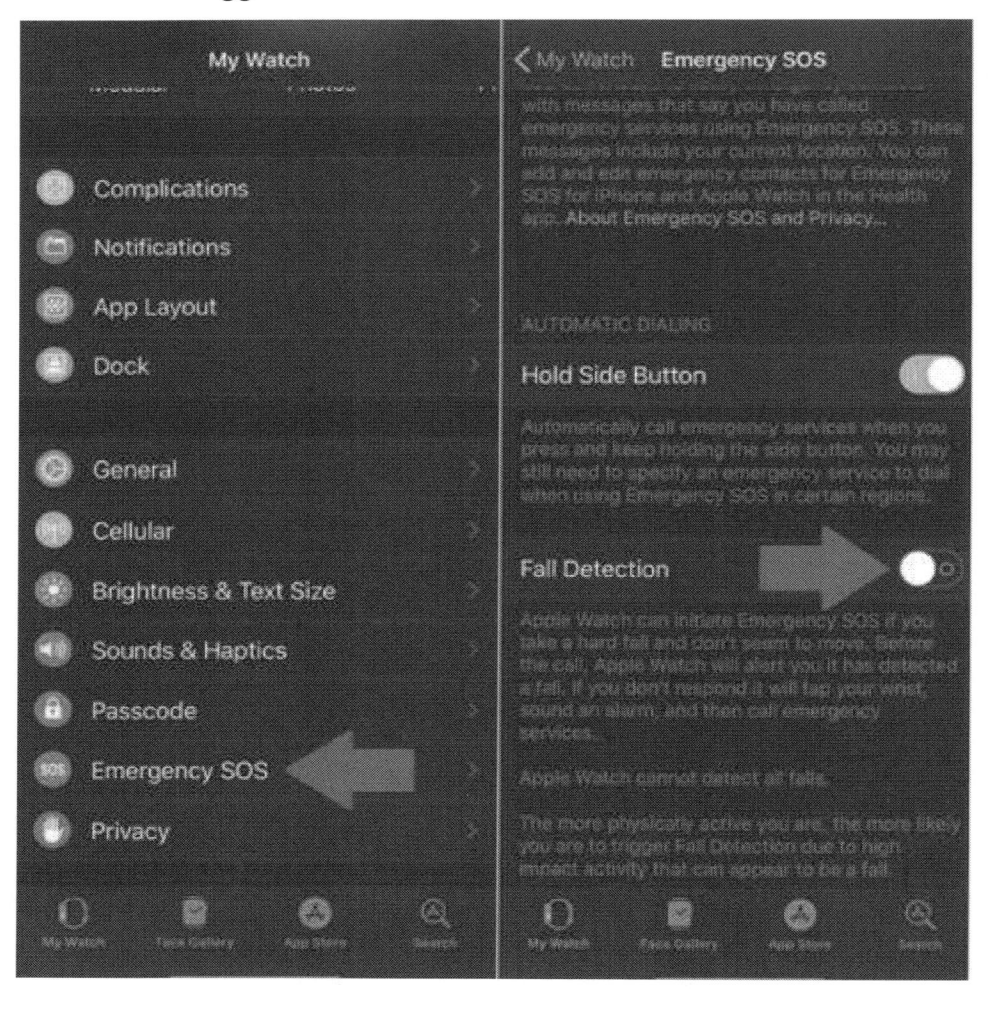

After enabling this feature on your phone, follow the steps below to enable it on your Apple Watch for a more accurate read:

- Open the Settings app on your watch.
- Click on **SOS**.
- Click on **Fall Detection**.
- Then click on **Fall Detection** to enable it.

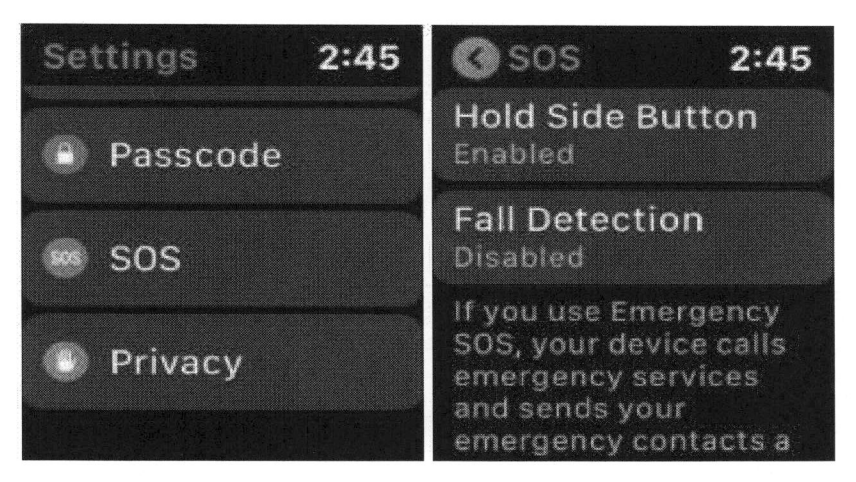

- Click on **Confirm**.
- Click on **Medical ID** to ensure that your contact details are well synced.

Set Up Your Medical ID

Your Medical ID provides first responders access to your critical medical information without needing your passcode. The ID contains details like your medical conditions, allergies, and emergency contacts.

- Click on the **Summary** tab in the Health app on your iPhone.
- Click on your profile picture at the top right side of your screen.

- Click on **Medical ID** under **Medical Details.**
- Click on **Edit** at the top right side of your screen.
- Toggle on **Show When Locked** if you want your ID accessible on the lock screen.
- Turn on **Share During Emergency Call** to share your Medical ID with the emergency team.

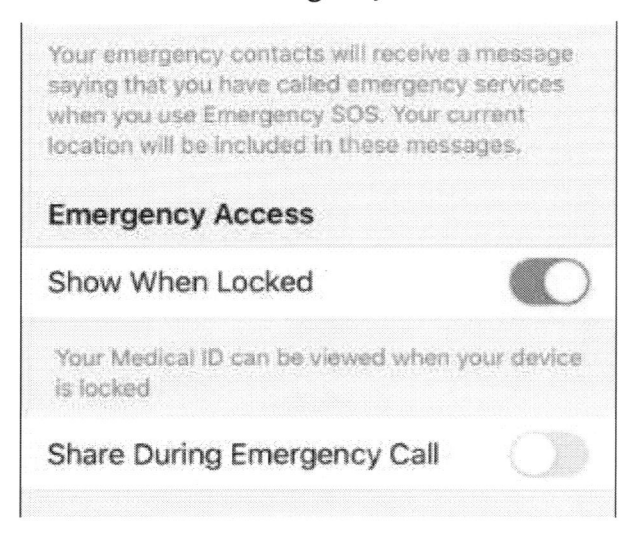

```
Your emergency contacts will receive a message
saying that you have called emergency services
when you use Emergency SOS. Your current
location will be included in these messages.
```

Emergency Access

Show When Locked

Your Medical ID can be viewed when your device is locked

Share During Emergency Call

- Then input details like your date of birth, blood type, and allergies.
- Tap **Done** to save.

Edit Emergency Contacts

Your watch will send a message to your emergency contacts when it detects a hard fall and has placed a call to emergency services. Here is how to set up your emergency contacts:

- Click on the **Summary** tab in the Health app on your iPhone.

- Click on your profile picture 👤 at the top right side of your screen.
- Click on **Medical ID** under **Medical Details.**
- Click on **Edit** at the top right side of your screen.
- Scroll to Emergency Contacts and tap ➕ beside **Add Emergency Contact.**
- Click on a contact and select your relationship with the contact.

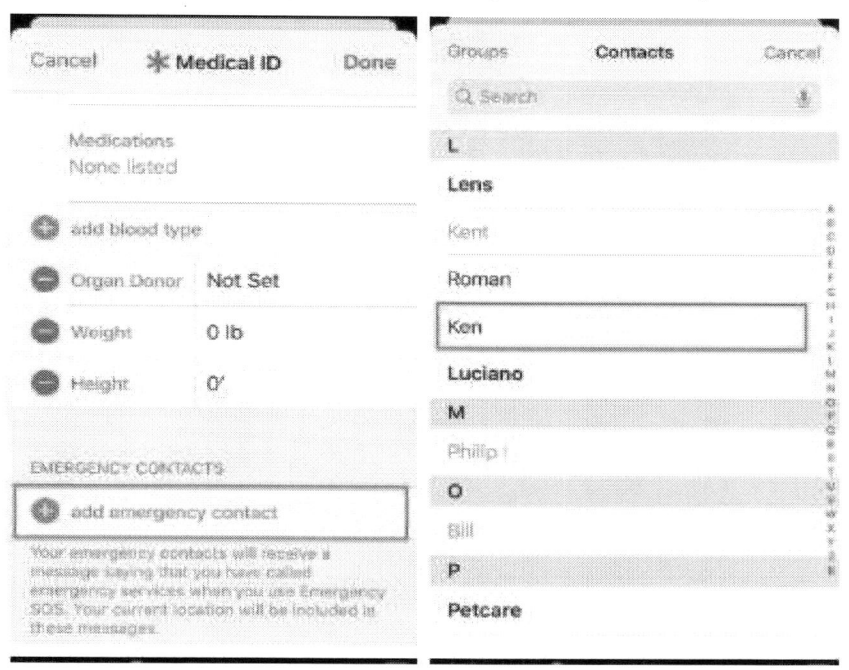

- Tap ➖ beside a contact to remove the person as your emergency contact, then tap **Delete.**
- Click on **Done** to save the details.

Make an Emergency Call

When your watch detects a hard fall, it rings an alarm asking if to contact Emergency services. To make the call,

- Drag the Emergency SOS slider in the alert.

End the Call

- Click on the end call button.
- Then tap **Yes** on the **End Call** screen.

Call Emergency Services

To call emergency services at any time even without the watch detecting a hard fall, follow the steps below:

- Press and hold the side button of your watch until you see the Emergency SOS slider on your screen.
- Keep holding the side button until an alarm sounds, and a countdown begins. Alternatively, you may drag the slider to the right to begin the call.
- At the end of the countdown, your watch will instantly place a call to emergency services.

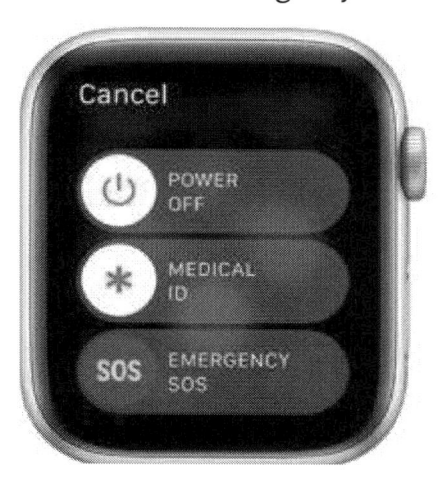

Stop Sharing Your Location

The Apple Watch shares your location with your emergency contact as well as the emergency team. During this time, you will receive a reminder every four hours. Click on **Stop Sharing** in the notification to stop sending your location to the emergency team and your contact.

Disable Automatic Dialing

By default, pressing down on the side button will call emergency services. To disable this, follow the steps below

- Launch the Apple Watch app on your phone and navigate to the **My Watch** tab.
- Click on **Emergency SOS.**
- Then toggle off **Hold Side Button.**

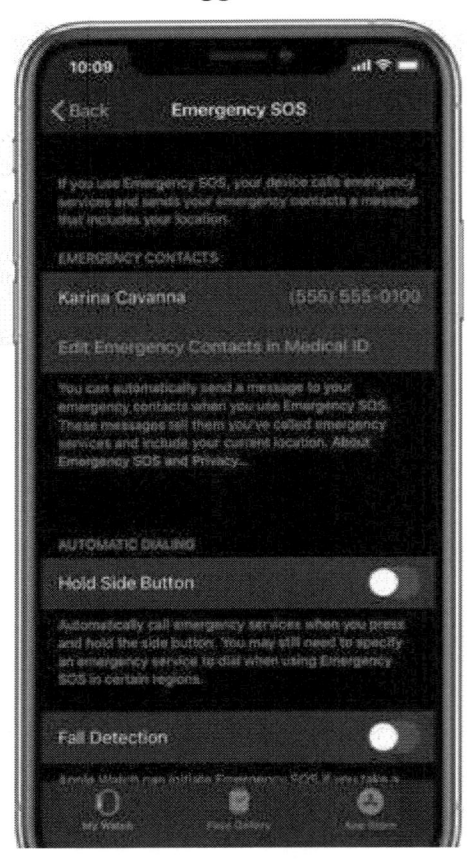

Note: even with this setting turned off, you can still make calls using the Emergency SOS slider.

Chapter 12: Track Your Sleep on Apple Watch

The Apple Watch does not have its own tracking app. However, there are different apps that you can download on your watch to help you track your sleep patterns and habits. With these third-party apps, all you need to do is to wear your watch to bed, and the app will monitor your sleep, tell how deeply you sleep as well as how long you sleep. These details are then transferred to your iPhone to help you keep track.

Download Sleep Tracker

You will need to download the sleep tracker to your iPhone.

- Open the Watch app on your paired iPhone.
- Click on **App Store.**
- Then click on **Discover Watch Apps on iPhone** and tap the search icon.
- Enter the name of a sleep tracker or just input **'sleep tracker'** in the search field.
- Click on **Get** for free apps or on the Price button to download and install paid apps.

Peradventure you have a sleep tracker app on your iPhone, all you need to do is to install the app on your watch.

- Open the Watch app on your paired iPhone. Go to the app and click on the **Install** button, and the app will move to your watch.

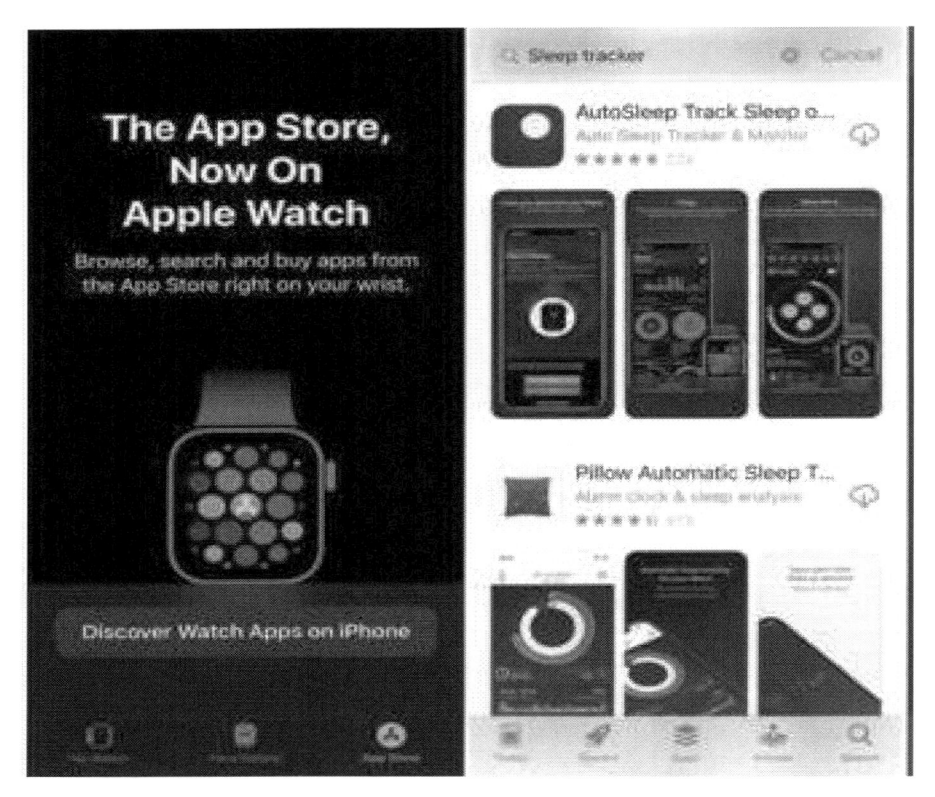

AutoSleep Tracker

This is one of the sleep tracking apps available on the app store. The app automatically tracks and records your sleep time. If you do not wear your watch while sleeping, the app will use your iPhone and only record the time you spent sleeping.

If you wear your watch to bed, it will use the watch sensors to tell when you slept. It will also monitor your heart rate as well as your body movement to give a sleep score in the morning.

You will need to let the app know when you typically go to bed and when you wake up. You may also manually click on the **Lights Off** button on the app to alert the app that you are going to sleep.

- Open the AutoSleep Tracker app on your watch and tap **Light Off**

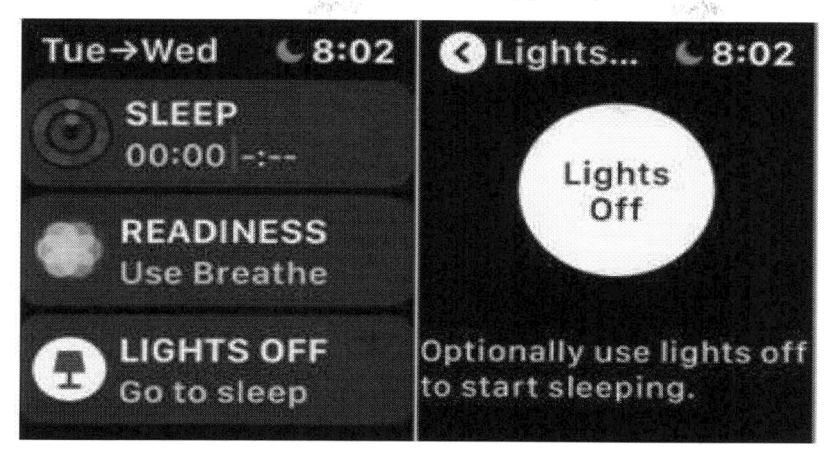

AutoSleep Data Tracking

To view your sleep data on your watch,

- Open the AutoSleep app, then swipe down on the screen to see more sleep details.

Pillow App

This is another sleep tracking app that can tell if you talk, snore, or make other noises while sleeping. The app is also able to track power naps and other short-time rest.

Before you go to bed, you will need to manually activate the sleep tracker by clicking on the **Start** button. When you do this for the first time, the app will prompt to know the item you want to track, like naps, sounds, etc. when you wake in the morning, launch the app on your watch and press hard on the Stop button to stop the timer. You may also press **Snooze** if you intend to continue the timer later.

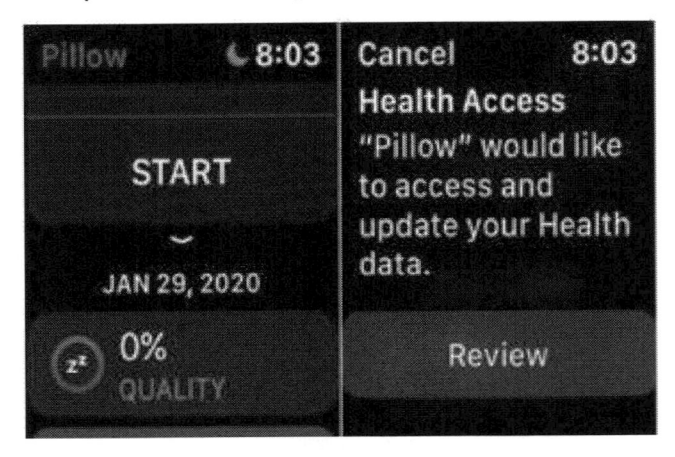

- Swipe down on the app screen to view the quality of your sleep for the previous nights. Swipe again to view the amount of time you spent in bed versus the time you spent asleep. You will also see the time you spent in each sleep cycle.

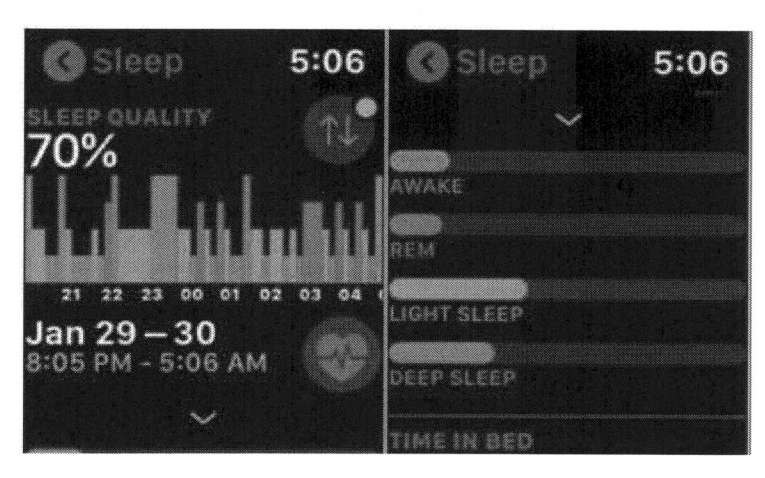

Sleep+ +

Yet another sleep tracker that you can use on your Apple Watch.

- Open the app on your Apple watch and click on **Start Manual Night** once its bedtime.
- Click on **Stop Sleeping** to stop recording.
- The app will show the amount of time you were in bed, an analysis of your sleeping pattern as well as a percentage measurement of how restless you were while sleeping.

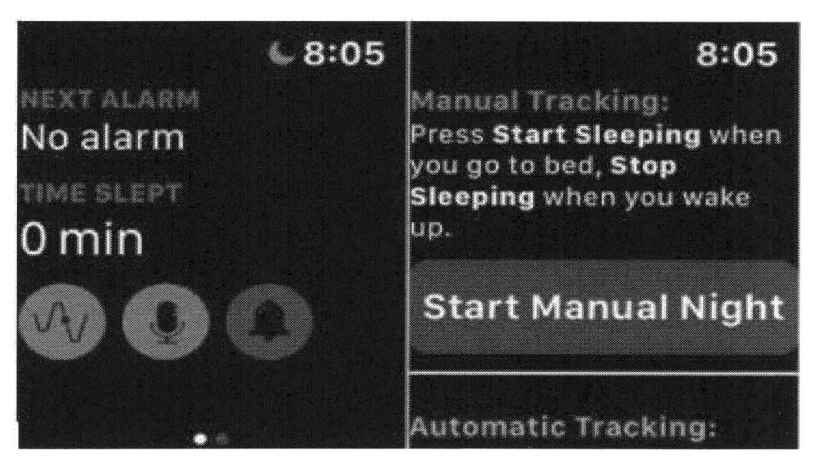

Chapter 13: The Noise App

This app helps to monitor noises in your surrounding and alert you if the noise volume in your environment can cause harm to your hearing.

Set Up the Noise App on the Apple Watch

The first step to using this feature is setting it up

- Open the Settings app on the watch and click on **Noise.**
- Click on **Environmental Sound Levels** and toggle on **Measure Sound.**
- Return to the previous screen and click on **Noise Notification.**
- Then click on a decibel level that you desire. Click on **Off** to disable noise notification.

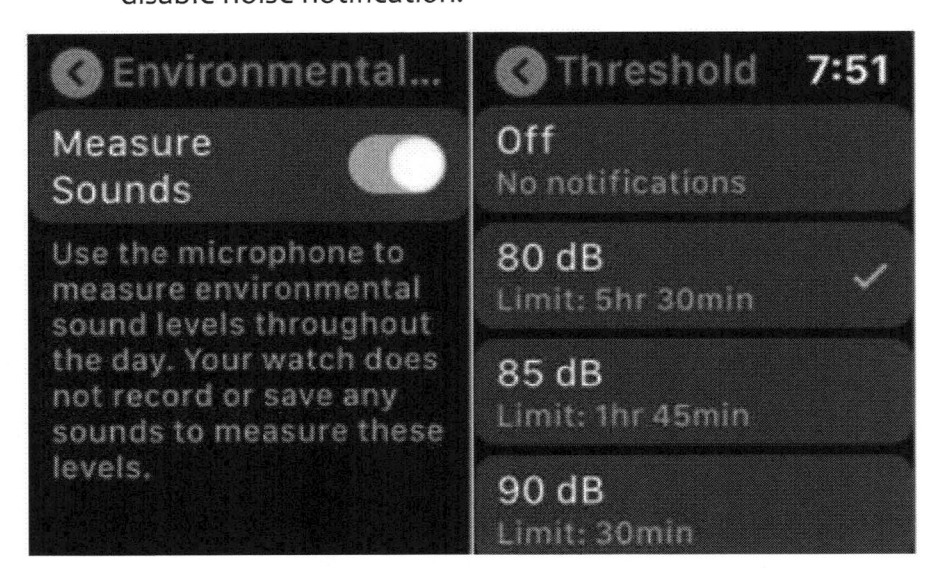

Enable/ Disable Noise Notification on iPhone

Here is how to activate the noise notification on your iPhone.

- Open the Watch app on your iPhone and click on the **My Watch** tab.
- Click on **Noise,** then click on **Noise Threshold.**
- Click on a decibel level that you desire. Click on **Off** to disable noise notification.

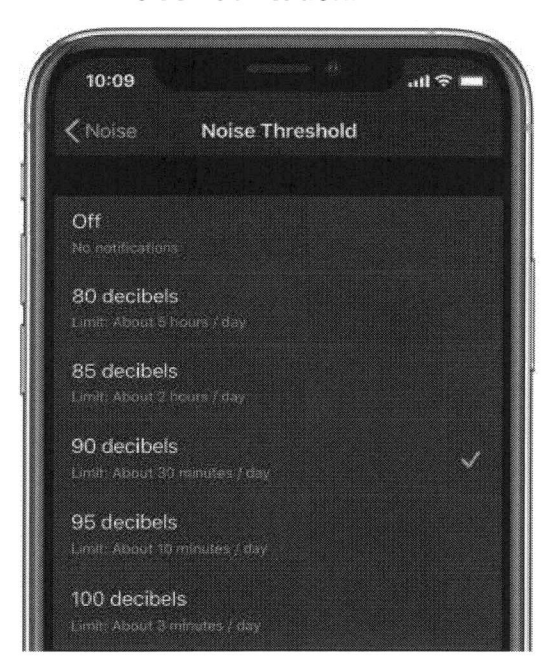

Monitor Noise on the Apple Watch

- Open the Noise app on your watch.
- Click on **Enable** to begin monitoring.

View Information about Environmental Sound Levels

To know more about environmental sound levels,

- Launch the Health app on your phone.
- Click on **Browse,** click on **Hearing,** then click on **Environmental Sound Levels.**

Disable or Enable Noise Measuring

- Open the Settings app ⚙ on the watch and click on **Noise.**
- Click on **Environmental Sound Levels,** then toggle off **Measure Sound.**

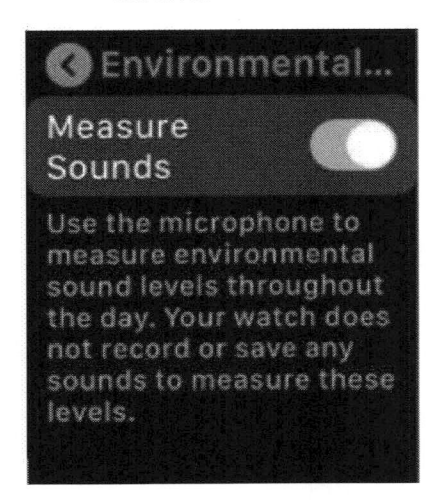

To do this on the iPhone,

- Open the Watch app on your phone and click on the **My Watch** tab.
- Click on **Noise,** then toggle off **Environmental Sound Measurements.**

Chapter 14: Cycle Tracking

The Cycle Tracking app allows you to monitor your menstrual cycles.

Setup Cycle Tracking on iPhone

- Launch the Health app on your phone.
- Click on the **Browse** tab at the bottom of your screen.
- Click on **Cycle Tracking,** then click on **Get Started.**
- Fill in the requested details like the date of your last period and the typical length of each menstrual cycle.
- Once done, scroll to the bottom of your screen and tap **Options**.
- Then toggle on or off features like Fertile Window Prediction, Log Sexual Activity, etc.

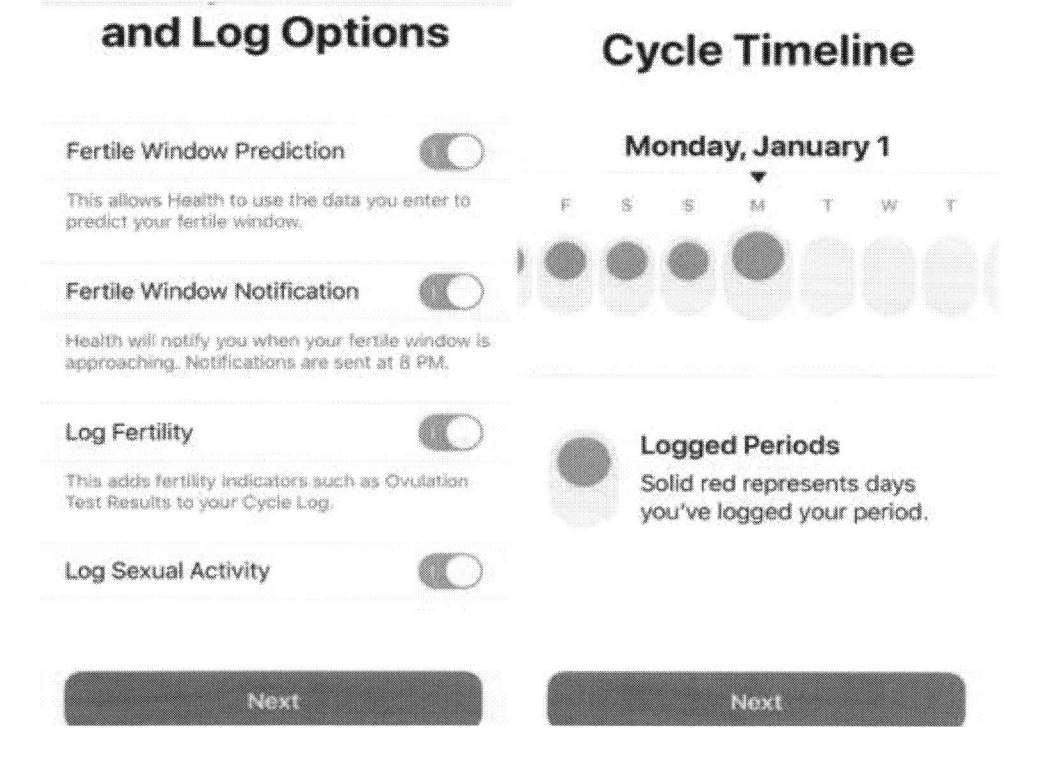

Track Your Menstrual Cycles

Here is how to record and track your cycle.

- Open the Cycle tracking app on your Apple Watch.
- Then log your period. Assign different colors for different stages.

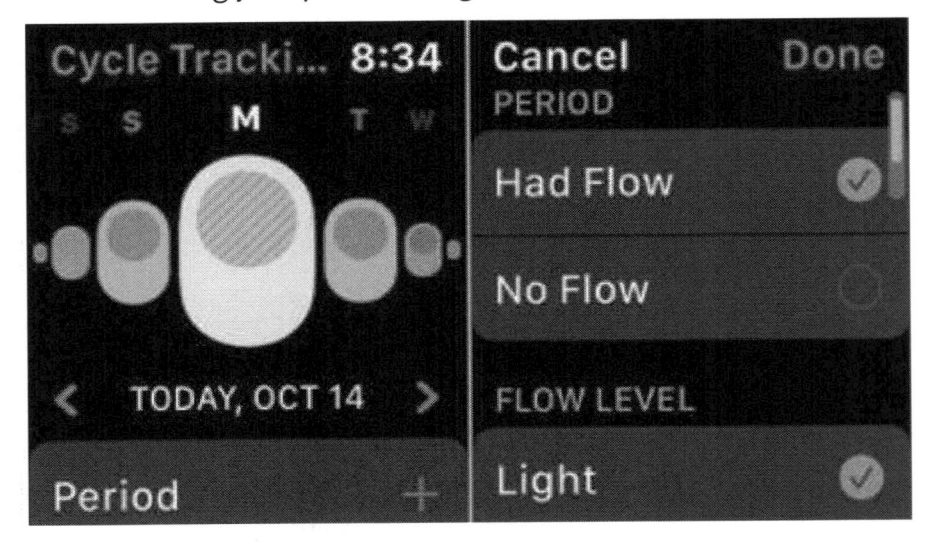

Chapter 15: Basic Settings

Power Off Apple Watch

- Press and hold the side button until you see the option to power off your device.
- Pull the **Power Off** slider to the right to power off your watch.

Note that you will be unable to power off the watch while it is connected to power.

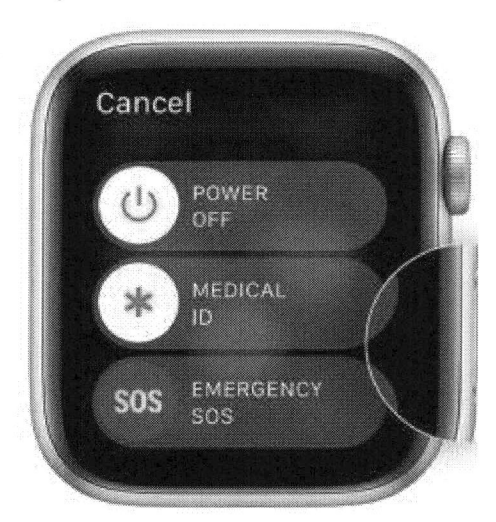

Force restart Your Watch

A force restart is helpful if your watch is completely frozen. To do this,

- Hold down both the digital crown and the side button for a minimum of ten seconds, until the Apple logo shows you on your screen.

Unlock Your Mac with Apple Watch

To unlock your Mac with your watch, you first need to activate the feature:

- Tap the Apple icon at the top left side of your Mac screen.

- Click on **System Preferences** from the drop-down list.

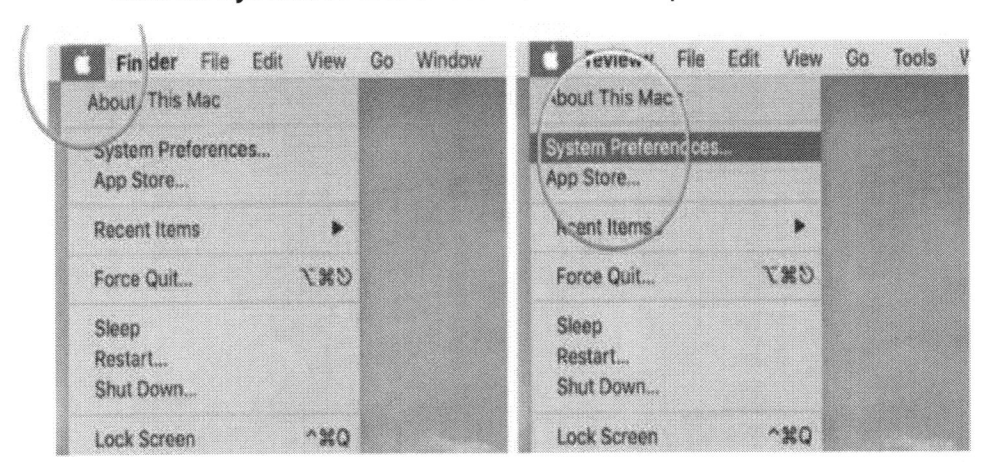

- Click on **Security & Privacy,** then click on **General.**
- Now enable the option for **Use your Apple Watch to unlock apps and your Mac.**

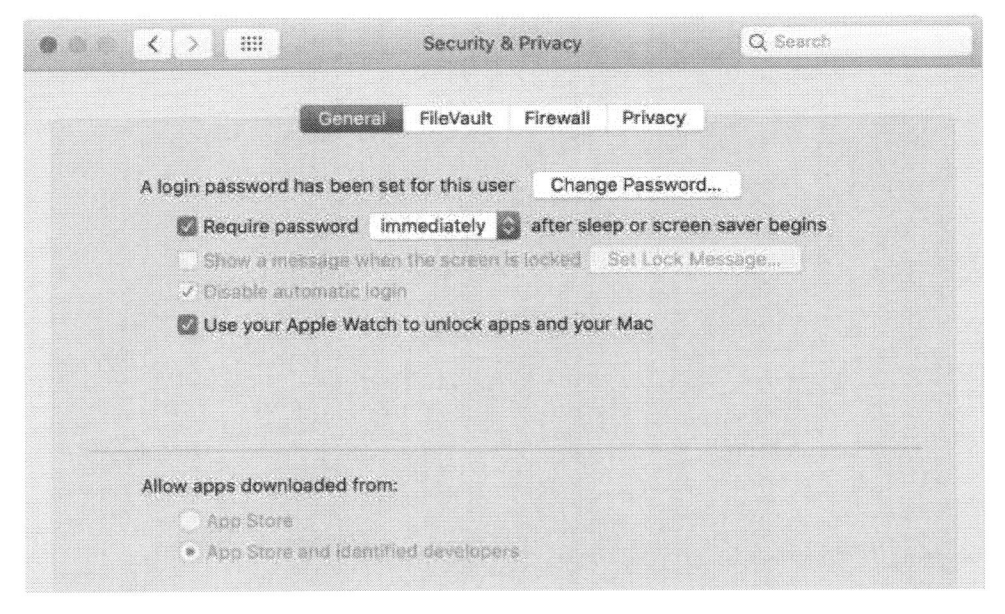

When next you start up your Mac while wearing your watch, your Mac will automatically log you in without prompting for a password.

Change Apple Watch Bands

To change the band,

- Place your watch with the screen facing down.
- Press down the band release button at the back of your watch, then slide the band across to take it out.

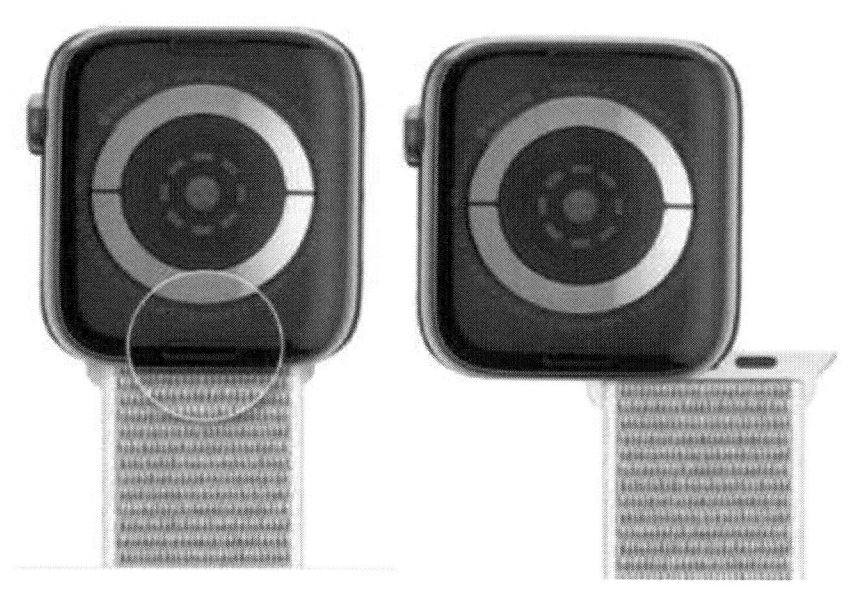

- Now slide in the new band until you hear a click sound.

View Your Calendar Events

To view events saved on your calendar,

- Open the Calendar app 10 on your watch.
- Turn the Digital Crown to browse through your events.
- Click on an event to view its details like invitee status, location, time, and note.

- Press firmly on your screen to change the daily views:
    - ✓ Tap **Up Next** to see your upcoming events for the current week.
    - ✓ Tap **Today** to see your planned event for the current day.
    - ✓ Tap **List** to show all your planned events from yesterday up till six days from the current day.
    - ✓ To view your events for a whole month, tap < at the upper left corner of any daily calendar.
    - ✓ Click on the monthly calendar to go back to Today's view.
    - ✓ Swipe right or left in the Today view to see the next day or the previous day. Or turn the Digital Crown while in the list view to see another day.
    - ✓ Press firmly on your screen and tap **Today** to return to the current day and time.

View a monthly calendar.

Turn to scroll events.

Firmly press to switch the daily view.

Set Default City for the Weather App

Here is how to set your default location:

- Launch the Watch app on your phone and click on **My Watch**.
- Click on **Weather,** then click on **Default City.**

Organize Your App

Here is how to rearrange your home screen in a layout that suits you:

- Launch the Watch app on your phone and click on **My Watch**.
- Click on **App Layout,** then drag an app icon to the new location.

You can also do this directly on your watch:

- Press the digital crown to return to the home screen.
- If your watch screen is in the list view, force press the display, then select **Grid View.**
- Press down on an app until the apps begin to jiggle, then drag the app to the new position.

Chapter 16: Walkie- Talkie on Apple Watch

The Walkie-Talkie app allows you to talk real-time with another person using your Apple Watch. The feature is a replicate of the old-fashioned walkie-talkie. For this app to work, your friend also needs to have an Apple watch series one or later. You both need to set up the FaceTime app on your iPhone.

Enable or Disable Walkie-Talkie

Here is how to enable or disable the app

- Open the app .
- Then toggle on or off **Walkie-Talkie.**
- If you disabled the app and a friend tries to reach you, you will receive a notification asking if you will like to talk.

Add Friends to the App

- Launch the walkie-talkie app on your watch.
- Click on **Add Friends,** then select a contact.

- Wait for the friend to accept your invitation.

Remove a Friend

- Open the walkie-talkie app. Swipe left on the name of the friend, then click on ✕.
- Alternatively, open the Apple Watch app on your paired iPhone, click on **Walkie-Talkie,** tap **Edit,** tap ⊖ beside the friend you wish to remove, then click on **Remove.**

Accept Walkie-Talkie Invitation

When a friend sends an invite to connect via walkie-talkie, the notification will appear on your watch screen.

- Open the Notification and click on **Always Allow.**
- You can also find the invitation in the walkie-talkie app.

Start a Walkie-Talkie Conversation

- Open the walkie-talkie app and click on a friend.
- Click and hold down the talk button while you say something. If your screen reads '**connecting,**' wait for the app to connect. Once it connects, your friend will be able to hear you and reply instantly.

Note: your friend always needs to wear the Apple watch as well as have the walkie-talkie app turned on to be able to receive alerts when you want to talk.

- To talk over the app, tap and hold the talk button. Release the button once you are done talking.
- Turn the digital crown to control the volume.

Chapter 17: Find My

Find Your iPhone with Apple Watch

If your paired iPhone ever goes missing, you can use the Apple watch to locate it.

- Press the digital crown to go to the watch face.
- Go to the Control Center – swipe up from the bottom of your screen.
- Then click on the iPhone icon. Once the icon changes to blue, your phone will begin to make pinging sound to help you locate it.

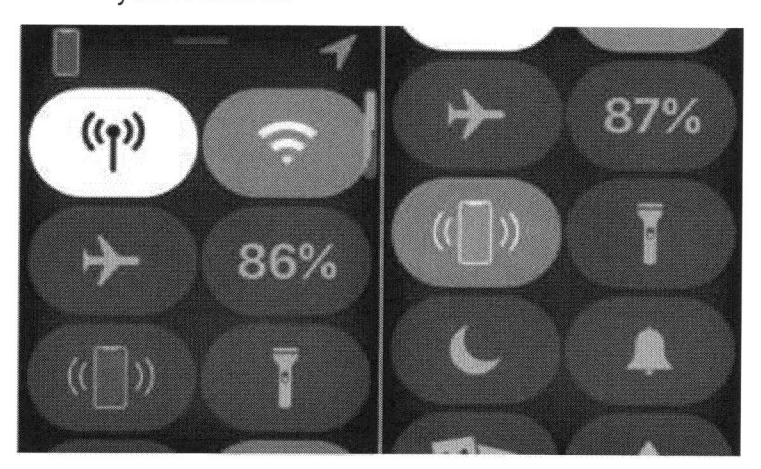

Find Your Apple Watch

Here is how to use the Find My app to locate a missing watch

- Open the Find My app on your paired phone.
- Click on **Devices,** then click on your Apple watch from the displayed list.

- On the next screen, click on the desired option: **Directions** to find your way to the watch, **Play a Sound** if you want the watch to make sounds, **Mark it as Lost** if you lost it in a public area, or **Erase It** to clear your data from the watch.

Mark Apple Watch As Lost

- Open the Find My app on your paired phone.
- Click on **Devices,** then click on your Apple watch from the displayed list.
- On the next screen, click on **Mark it as Lost.**

Chapter 18: Camera App

You can do a lot with the camera app on your watch like remotely take pictures on your iPhone using the Apple Watch as a remote control.

Take a Photo

To have Siri take a photo of you,

- Say something like, "Take a Photo."

Remotely Take a Photo on Your Phone

To take a photo with your iPhone using the watch, you need to ensure that both devices are within normal Bluetooth range.

- Position your phone to capture the shot, then launch the camera app on your watch.
- Click on the timer at the bottom right side of your watch to set a timer of three seconds. Alternatively, click on the shutter button to capture your photo right away.

Take a Live Photo

Here is how to capture a live photo on your Apple watch.

- Position your phone to capture the shot, then launch the camera app on your watch.
- Press firmly on your watch screen until a pop-up menu appears, then click on **Live**.

Use a Different Camera

To change from the front-facing camera to the rear-facing camera on your iPhone and vice versa,

- Position your phone to capture the shot, then launch the camera app on your watch.
- Press firmly on your watch screen until a pop-up menu appears, then click on **Flip**.

Use a Different Camera Mode

- Launch the Camera app on your phone, then swipe through the available options until you find the one that you want.

View Your Shots on Apple Watch

To view the photos that you captured on your watch,

- Launch the camera app on your watch.
- Then click on the thumbnail at the bottom left side of your screen.
- Swipe right or left to view your images.
- Turn the digital crown to zoom your photo.
- Double click on a photo to have it fill the screen.
- Click on your screen once to show or hide the shot count and the **Close** button.
- Tap **Close** to exit.

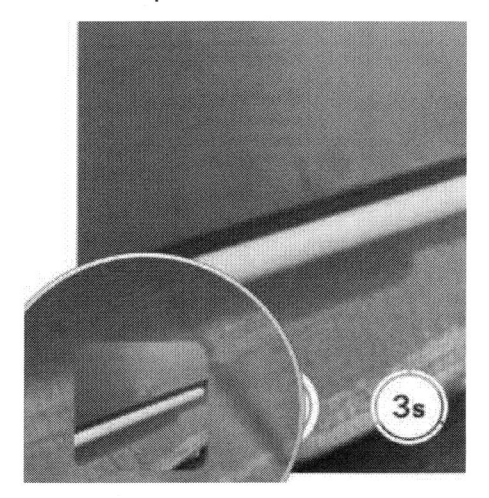

Chapter 19: Photo App

Browse Photos

You can access some photos stored on your iPhone on the Apple Watch, like all the photos that you tagged as Favorites on the iPhone.

- Launch the Watch app on your phone and click on **My Watch** tab at the bottom of your screen.
- Click on **Photos,** then click on **Synced Album** and select the album you wish to view on your watch.
- If there is one picture in a selected album that you do not want on your watch, open the Gallery app on your phone and move the picture from the synced album.

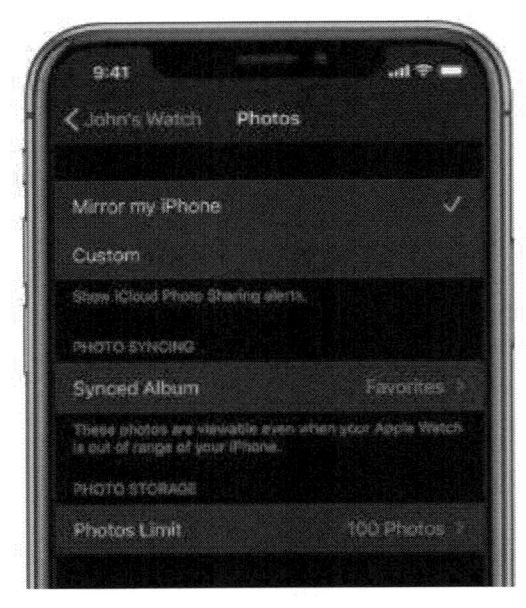

View Photos on the Photos App

- Open the Photos app on your watch to view thumbnails of the images in the synced album.

- Swipe right or left to browse through them.
- Click on an image to open it.
- Turn the digital crown or tap your screen to zoom in on an image.

View Life Photo on Apple Watch

- Open the Photo app on your watch and check for photos that have the Live photo icon on the bottom right side of a photo.
- Touch and hold the photo to view it.

Show a Photo on The Watch Face

You can use any of your pictures on the watch face. To do this,

- Open the desired picture in the Photos app.
- Press down on the photo until you see a pop-up.
- Then click on **Create Watch Face.**

Limit Photo Storage on Apple Watch

Your Apple Watch, just like other similar devices, has limited storage space. You may limit the number of pictures that you can store on the watch, to make room for other content.

- Launch the Watch app on your phone and click on **My Watch** tab at the bottom of your screen.
- Click on **Photos,** then click on **Photos Limit** to set the limit.

View Number of Photos Stored on Your Watch

Below is how to see how many photos that are stored on your watch.

- Launch the Settings app on your watch.

- Click on **General,** then click on **About** to view this information.

To view this on your phone,

- Launch the Watch app on your phone and click on **General** at the bottom of your screen. Then click on **About.**

To view the amount of space used for your pictures,

- Launch the Settings app on your watch.
- Click on **General,** then click on **Usage.**

Take a Screenshot

Before you can take a screenshot on your Apple Watch, you need to enable the option.

- Launch the Settings app on your watch.
- Click on **General,** then click on **Screenshots** and toggle on **Enable Screenshots.**
- Then press the side button and the digital crown to capture your watch screen.
- The screenshots are saved in the Photos app on your iPhone.

Chapter 20: Apple Watch App Store

The Apple Watch has its own app store and is no longer dependent on the app store of the paired iPhone. You can search for apps and download apps right on the watch. The first thing is to ensure that you are on the latest WatchOS, then follow the guides below to set up the app store and customize your settings

Customize App Store Settings on Apple Watch

You can also customize these settings directly on your watch.

- Open the Settings app and click on **App Store.**
- Toggle on or off **Automatic Updates** and **Automatic Downloads.**

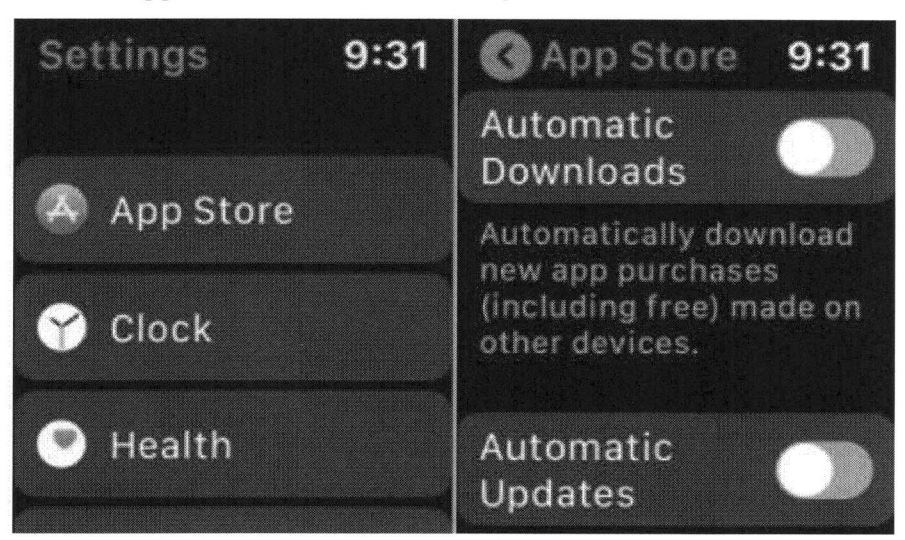

Customize App Store Settings on iPhone

You need to customize some settings for the app store on your iPhone.

- Launch the Watch app on your paired iPhone.

- You can set the watch to have all the apps that you download on your iPhone. To configure this, click on the **General** tab, then toggle on **Automatic App Install.**
- To install apps available on your other Apple devices like iPad, click on **My Watch** at the bottom of your screen, click on **App Store,** then toggle on **Automatic Downloads.**
- Toggle on **Automatic Updates** if you want the downloaded apps to be automatically updated.

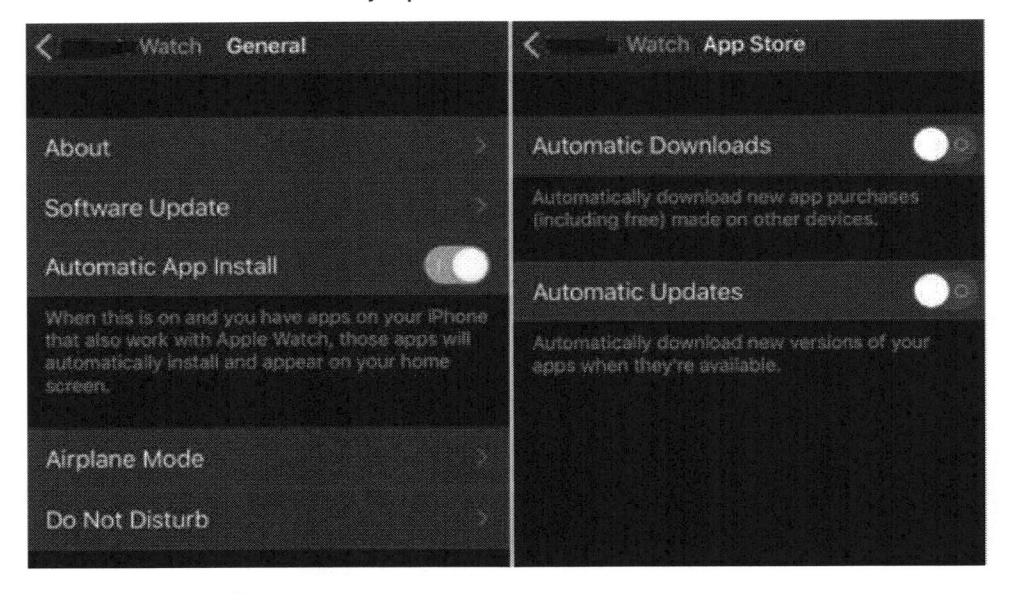

View App Details

Here is how to view app details like reviews, ratings, version history, etc

- Open the App Store on your watch and click on an app.
- Swipe down to view the app description and other details.

Download Apps to the iPhone and Watch Simultaneously

Having enabled the Automatic Downloads and App Install options, any watch-compatible app you download on your iPad or iPhone will also appear on your Apple Watch.

- Open the Watch app on your iPhone and click on the **App Store** icon. Click on **Discover Watch Apps on iPhone.**
- You will then see all watch-compatible apps on the iPhone app store. Click on an app to download it, and the app will appear on your phone and watch.

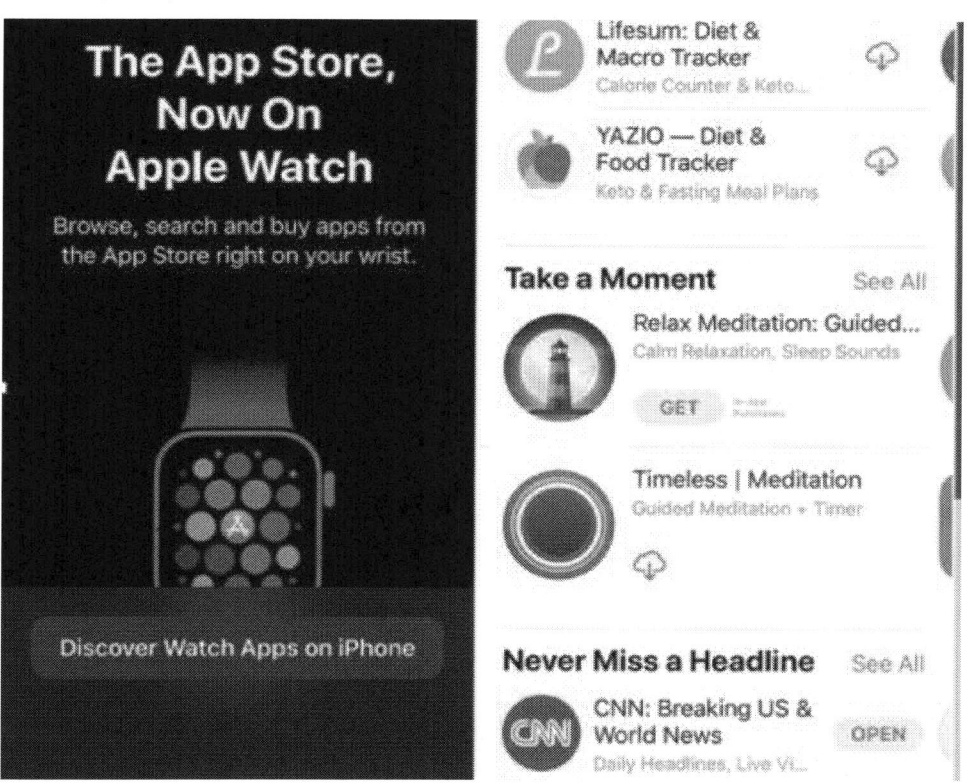

App Store on Apple Watch

Here is how to use the app store on your watch

- Press the digital crown to go home. Then click on the App Store icon .
- Turn the digital crown to navigate through the featured apps.
- Click on a category or click on **See All** underneath a collection to view all the apps for that section.
- Tap **Get** to download the app or click on the price to buy a paid app. If the download button appears instead of the price, it means you have previously purchased the app and can re-download it at no cost.
- Use the search button at the top of your screen to search for a specific app. Click on **Dictation** to dictate your search term, or click on **Scribble,** then use your finger to draw each letter of the search term, then tap **Done.**

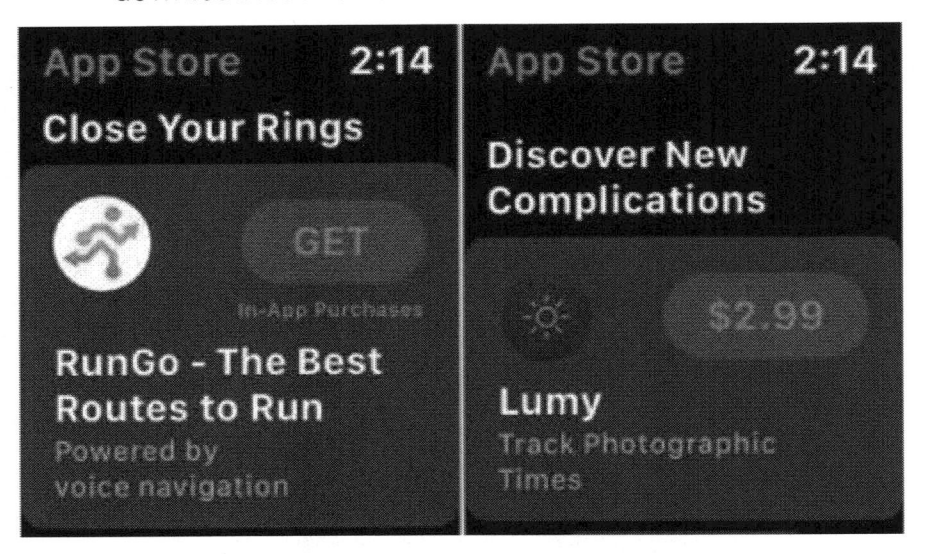

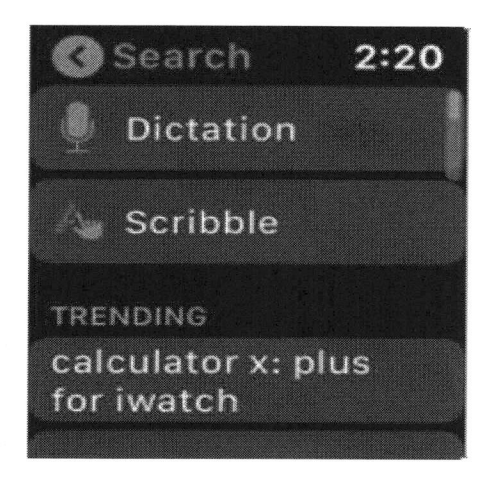

View Purchased Apps

To view the apps that you purchased,

- Open the App Store on your watch and swipe down.
- Click on **Account.** Click on **Purchased,** then click on **My Purchases** to see all downloaded apps.

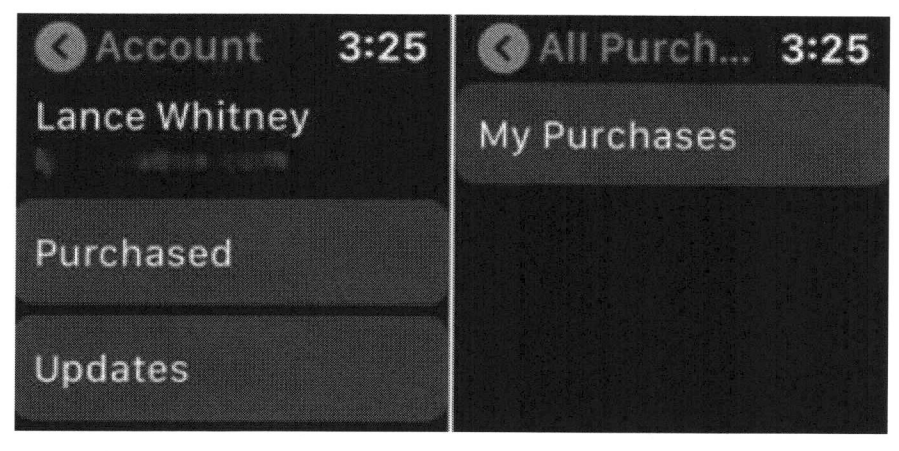

Delete Apps from Watch

Here is how to delete apps directly on the Apple Watch.

- Press the digital crown to go to your home screen.

- If your home screen is in Grid view, gently press down on any of the app icons until they begin to wiggle, then click on the X button above the app that you want to delete. Then click on the **Delete** icon to remove the app. Press the Digital Crown to escape the wiggle mode.
- If your watch's home screen is in **List View,** swipe down to the app you want to delete, then swipe left on the app. Click on the trash can icon . Then click on **Delete App.**

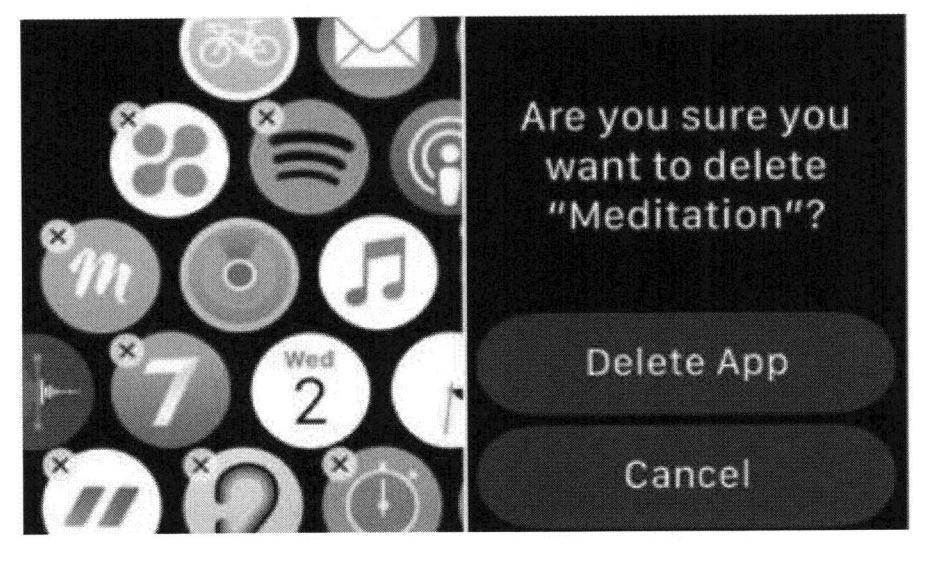

Chapter 21: Apple Pay

Apple Pay allows you to securely and conveniently make payments in stores and online using your Apple Watch. First, you need to set up this feature on your iPhone before it can work on the Apple Watch.

Set Up Apple Pay

- Launch the Apple Watch app on your phone and navigate to the **My Watch** tab.
- Click on **Wallet & Apple Pay.**
- The next screen will display all the cards that are active on your other Apple devices as well as cards that you removed recently. To add these cards, click on **Next** beside the card and then type in the CVV for the card.
- To add other cards, click on **Add Card,** then follow the instruction on your screen.

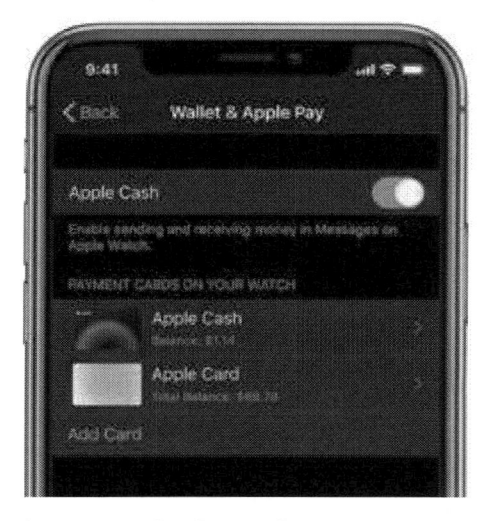

Choose Default Card

- Launch the Apple Watch app on your phone and navigate to the **My Watch** tab.
- Click on **Wallet & Apple Pay.**
- Scroll down and click on **Default Card,** then choose the card of your choice.

Remove a Card From Apple Pay

- Click on the Wallet app on your watch, then click on the card you want to delete.
- Press firmly on the card, then click on **Remove Card.**

Follow the steps below to do this on your iPhone

- Launch the Apple Watch app on your phone and navigate to the **My Watch** tab.
- Click on **Wallet & Apple Pay.**
- Click on the card, then click on **Remove This Card.**

Pay With the Apple Watch

Here is how to make payment with the Apple Watch

- Double press the side button to display your default card.
- Position the Apple Watch near the contactless reader until you feel a soft tap.
- Enter your PIN if prompted to complete the payment.

To pay using a different card,

- Double press the side button then swipe until you get to the card you wish to use.
- Once the card shows on your screen, place the watch near the contactless reader until you feel a soft tap. Press the Digital Crown to return to your watch face.

Find Device Account Number for a Card

When you complete a payment using your watch, the merchant is sent the device account number of the card along with the payment. Here is how to view the last four digit of this account number

- Launch the Apple Watch app on your phone and navigate to the **My Watch** tab.
- Click on **Wallet & Apple Pay,** and then click on the card.

Modify Default Transaction Details

To change your in-app transaction details like your phone number, shipping address, email or default card, follow the steps below:

- Launch the Apple Watch app on your phone and navigate to the **My Watch** tab.
- Click on **Wallet & Apple Pay.**
- Scroll down to **Transaction Defaults.** Click on an item to modify.

Chapter 22: Siri

Siri is the Apple virtual assistant that helps you to perform requested tasks.

Set Up Siri

- Open the Settings app ⚙ on your watch.
- Click on **Siri,** then toggle on **Hey Siri.**
- Also, toggle on **Press Digital Crown** to activate Siri by tapping the digital crown.

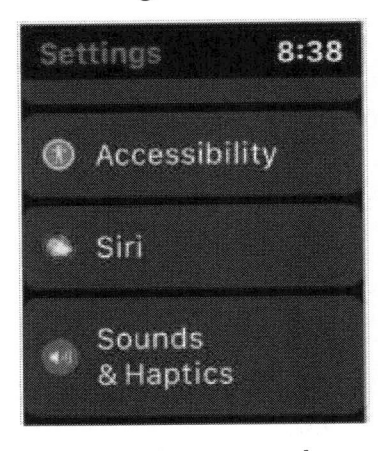

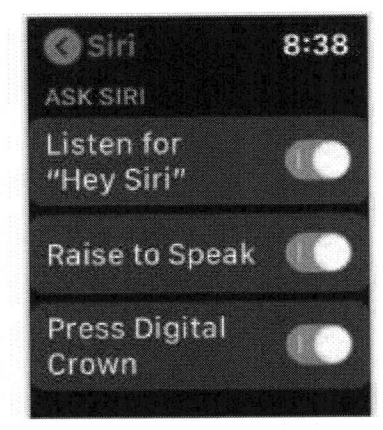

Enable Raise to Speak

This feature allows you to speak to Siri by raising your wrist. Here is how to enable it:

- Open the Settings app ⚙ on your watch.
- Click on **Siri,** then toggle on **Raise to Speak.**

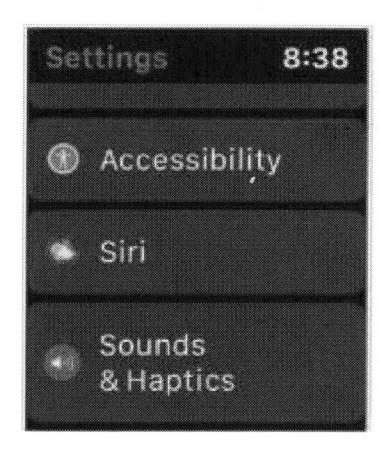

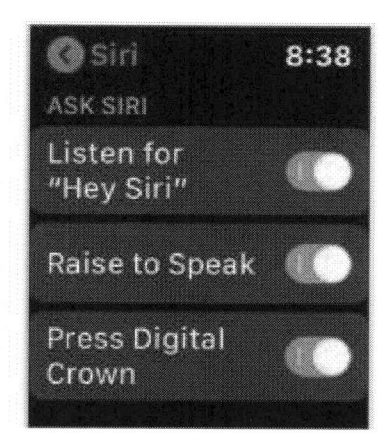

With this feature enabled, simply raise your wrist close to your mouth and begin to speak to Siri.

Manually Activate Siri

Another way to speak to Siri is

- Press down on the Digital Crown while you speak your command or question to Siri.

Hey Siri

Here is another way to speak to Siri

- Tap on your screen to wake your phone.
- Then start with Hey Siri, followed by your command or question.

Change Siri's Voice on Apple Watch

Siri responds to your question or command using vocal tones. Here is how to change the Siri's voice

- Launch the Settings app on your paired iPhone.
- Click on **Siri & Search.**
- Click on **Siri Voice** and choose the voice that you like.

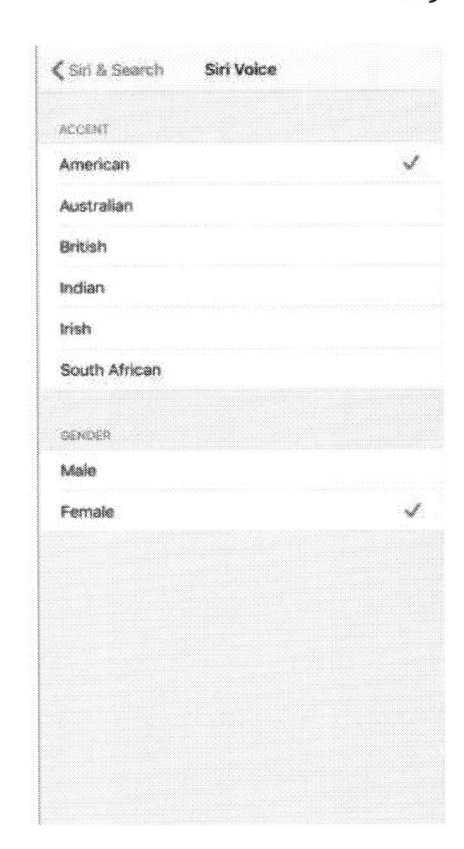

Disable Siri Voice on Apple Watch

Here is how to disable Siri on your Apple watch.

- Open the Settings app on your watch.
- Click on **Siri,** then toggle off **Hey Siri.**

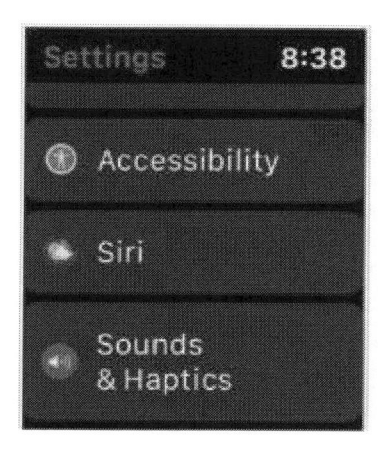

Use Handoff to Switch From Siri on Your Watch to Your Phone

The Handoff feature allows you to begin an action on your iPhone/ Apple Watch and complete the action on your Apple Watch/ iPhone, that is, starting action on one device and completing the action on another device. You may be unable to perform some actions on your watch owing to the size. Siri may then transfer your request to your phone. Enable this option with the steps below

- Launch the Apple Watch app on your phone and navigate to the **My Watch** tab.
- Click on **General,** and then toggle on **Enable Handoff**

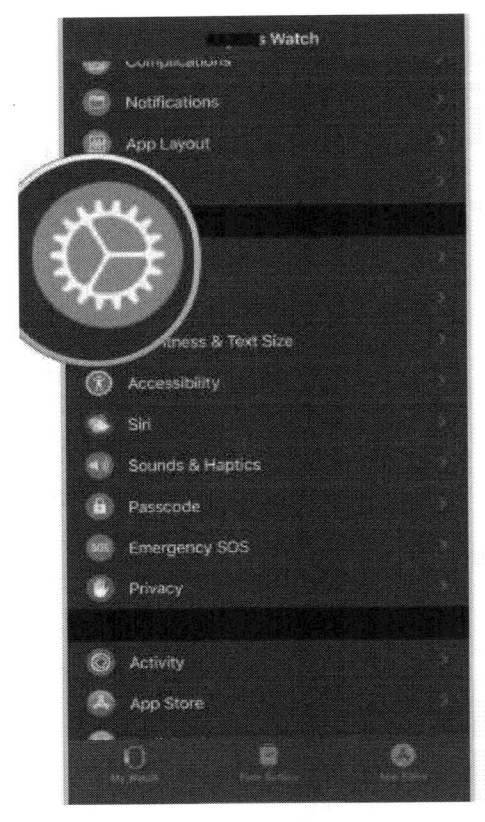

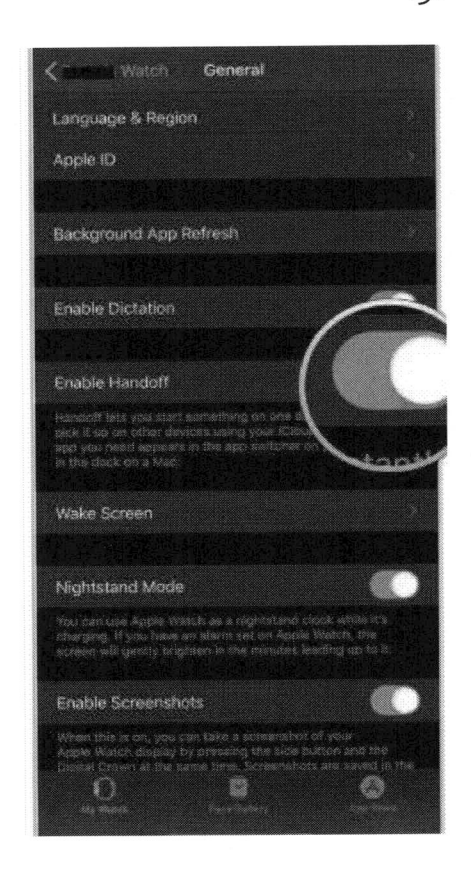

Set Up Siri Watch Face

Set up the Siri watch face to give you a customized Siri button on your watch face, that will pull in data from your photos, calendars, etc., providing you with details like upcoming weather.

- Click on your watch display or raise your wrist to activate your watch.
- Firmly press the screen of your watch.
- Then turn the Digital Crown or swipe to the left until you get to the end of your screen. Click on the + button.

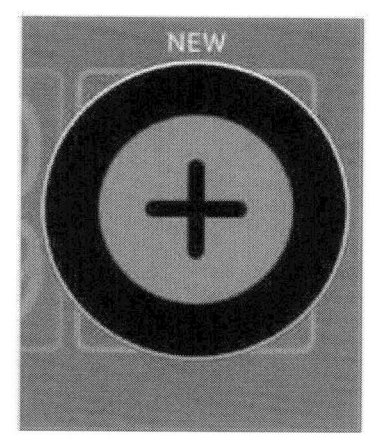

- Scroll through the list until you get to **Siri Watch Face.** Click on it.

Set Up Siri Watch Face on iPhone

For different options for the Siri Watch face, I will advise you to customize the watch face using your iPhone.

- Launch the Apple Watch app on your phone and navigate to the **Face Gallery** tab.
- Click on **Siri,** then tap the **Add** button.

- Click on **My Watch** tab and scroll to the left under **My Faces** section.
- Click on **Siri**. Select your **Top Right** and **Top Left** complications.
- Select your **Data Sources**.
- Then click on **Set as Current Watch Face** to start using.

Use Siri Watch Face

Here is how to use this watch face.

- Click on your watch display or raise your wrist to activate your watch.
- Click on the Siri button to begin using Siri.
- Turn the Digital Crown to view cards for an upcoming event, current weather, and lots more.
- Click on any of the cards to go to the corresponding watch app.

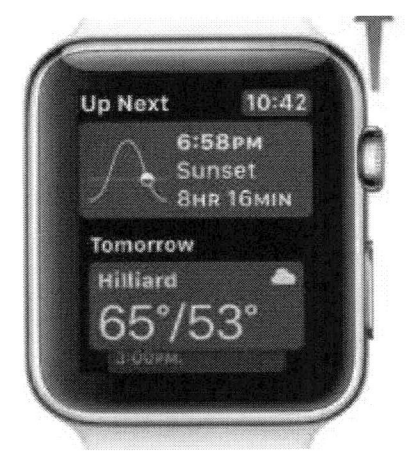

Chapter 23: Watch Faces

You can customize your watch face to have different looks and fit the moment. You can customize different watch faces to have different styles & colors or fit them with specific complications & features.

We will look at the different watch faces and how you can switch or tweak the watch faces.

The Face Gallery

This is the fastest and easiest way to view all the available watch faces. This feature also allows you to customize and add watch faces to your collection.

- Open the Apple Watch app on your iPhone, then click on **Face Gallery.**
- Click on a watch face, then click on a feature like style or color to customize it.
- To add complication to a watch face, click on a face, then click on a complication position like **Bottom, Top Right** or **Top Left.** Swipe to see all the available complications for that position, then click on the one that you like. Tap **Off** at the top of the list to disable complications for that position.
- After customizing the watch face, click on **Add.**

Add Complications on the Apple Watch

Complications are unique faces that are added to watch faces to pick things like the weather report, stock prices, and information from apps installed on the watch.

- Press the digital crown on your watch to go to the watch face.
- Press firmly on the screen then click on **Customize.**
- Swipe left till you get to the end. Every watch faces that offer complications are shown on the last screen.
- Click on a complication to select it, then rotate the digital crown to select a new complication like Heart rate.
- Tap the digital crown to record your changes, then click on the face again to switch to it.

Add Complications from Other Apps

Apart from built-in complications that displays information like news, weather, or stock, you can also add complications from other apps that you download from the app store. Here is how to make these complications available in the face customization screen:

- Open the Watch app on your iPhone and click on **My Watch** at the bottom of the screen.
- Then click on **Complications.**

Install a New Watch Face

Here is how to make your own collection of custom watch faces.

- Press the digital crown on your watch to go to the watch face, then press firmly on the screen.
- Swipe left till you get to the end. Then click on the **+ New** icon.
- Use the digital crown to navigate through the watch faces, then click on the one you want to add.

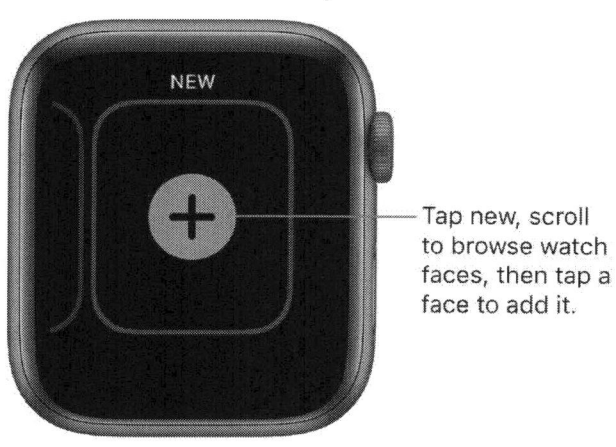

Tap new, scroll to browse watch faces, then tap a face to add it.

View Your Watch Face Collection

To arrange the order of the watch faces and have the frequently used ones readily available,

- Open the Watch app on your phone and click on **My Watch** at the bottom of your screen.
- Navigate to **My Faces** and browse through your collection.
- To reorder your watch faces to easily reach your favorite faces, click on **Edit,** then drag the ☰ icon beside a watch face and drag it to your desired position.

- Click on **Done** to save your changes.

Change Watch Faces

To change your current watch face, just swipe to the right or the left on your current watch face. Stop when you get to the face that you want to use.

Create Watch Faces with Photos

You can also use your personal photos to create a watch face. To do this,

- Open the Watch app on your iPhone and click on the **Face Gallery** tab at the bottom of the screen. Scroll to the **Photos** section, and you will find your favorite album as the default.
- Click on any of the watch faces on the screen to go to the customization screen.

- Then click on any of the customization options on the next screen.
    - ✓ **Synced Album** uses the photo album that you sync on your iPhone for the watch face.
    - ✓ **Photos** allow you to choose one or more pictures for the watch face.
    - ✓ **Dynamic** makes use of your new photos and photos from your recent memories.
- Click on your preferred option from the three options above and tap **Done** to save.

Delete Watch Faces Via iPhone

To delete a face using your iPhone,

- Open the Watch app on your phone and click on **My Watch** at the bottom of your screen.
- Navigate to **My Faces** and click on **Edit**.

139

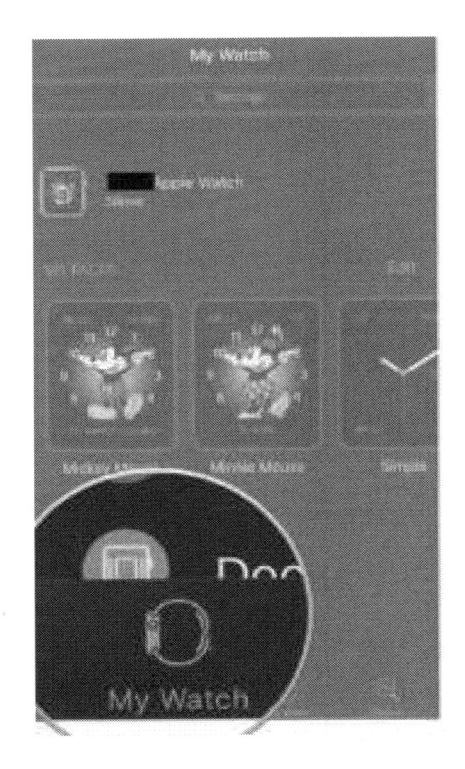

- Click on ⊖ beside the face you wish to delete, then click on **Remove.**

Delete a Face From Your Collection

- Press the digital crown on your watch to go to the watch face, then press firmly on the screen to display the watch faces.
- Scroll to the face you want to delete, then swipe up on the watch face and click on **Remove.**

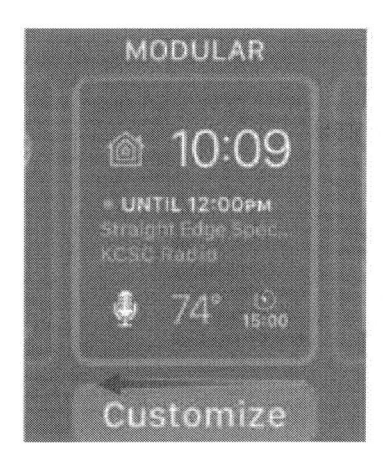

Make Your Watch Five Minutes Fast

You can manually set the time on your watch face to read five minutes faster than the current time. This has no effect on your notifications, alarms, or clocks from other countries.

- Open the Settings app on your watch.
- Click on **Time,** then click on **+0 min.**
- Now use the digital crown to change the time up to 59 minutes.

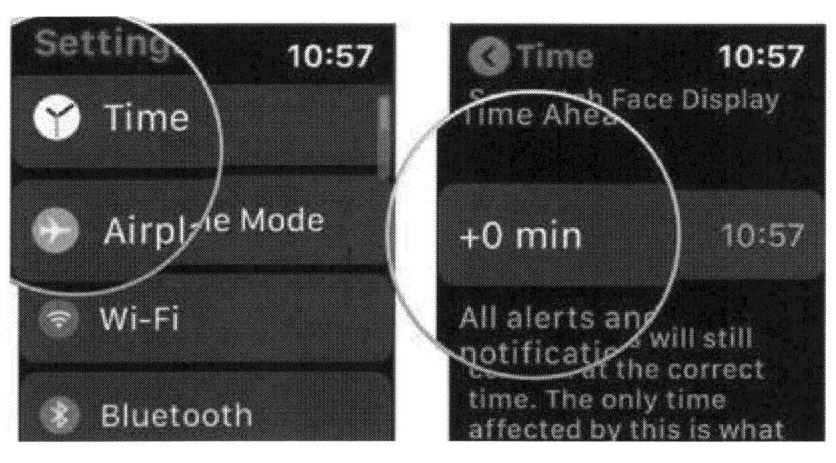

Chapter 24: Control Your Home with Apple Watch

The Home app offers you a safe way to automate and control compatible accessories like smart plugs, window shades, thermostats, cameras, and lots more.

When you first launch the Home app on your paired phone, the setup assistant will help you to create a home, and then you can begin to create rooms and add the accessories. Whatever you create on the iPhone will be available on your watch.

Add a New Scene or Accessory

You can access your favorite scenes and accessories on your watch. Follow the steps below to set an item as a favorite.

- Open the Home app on your phone and click on **Rooms.**
- Swipe to the right or left to find a scene or accessory, then press down on it.
- Make a swipe up, then enable **Include in Favorite.**

Control Smart Home Accessories

- Open the Home app on your watch.
- Swipe to a scene or an accessory and tap the icon, then modify your settings.

- Swipe to the left to view more options.
- Tap **Done** to go back to the accessories list.

Control Smart Home Scenes

- Open the Home app on your watch.
- Click on a scene to enable or disable.

View a Different Home

If you created more than one home on your iPhone, you can select the home that should show up on your watch.

- Open the Home app on your watch.
- Press hard on the screen display, then click on **Change Home** and select the one you want to see.

Chapter 25: Screen Display

Show Last Used App on Wake Screen

By default, when you move your wrist or lift your wrist, the watch will wake and display the time. But you can change the settings to show your last-used app before the watch went to sleep. To do this

- Open the Settings app on your watch and click on **General.**
- Click on **Wake Screen,** then toggle on **Wake Screen on Wrist Raise.**
- Scroll down to **On Screen Raise Show Last App** and select your desired option.

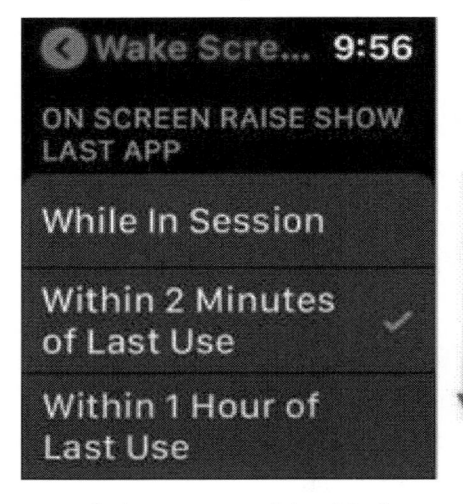

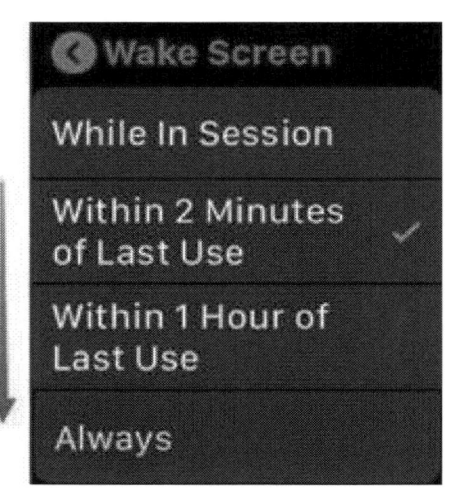

Here is how to enable this feature via your iPhone

- Open the Watch app on your phone and click on **My Watch** at the bottom of your screen.
- Click on **General,** then click on **Wake Screen.**
- Scroll down to **On Screen Raise Show Last App** and select your desired option.

Enable Always on Display

AOD always shows the time and watch face on your watch even when your wrist is down.

- Open the Settings app on your watch.
- Click on **Display and Brightness,** then click on **Always On.**
- Toggle on **Always On.**

- To hide details like heart rate, messages, calendar events ad so on when your wrist is down, toggle on **Hide Sensitive Complications.**

Wake the Watch Display

There are several ways to wake your watch:

- Press the digital crown or click on the watch display.
- Raise your wrist.
- Turn the digital crown upward. You will need to activate this option to use it.
    - ✓ Open the Settings app on your watch and click on **General.**
    - ✓ Click on **Wake Screen,** then click on **Wake Screen on Crown Up.**

Disable Wake Screen on Wrist Raise

If you do not want your watch screen awake when you raise your wrist, follow the steps below to disable the option

- Open the Settings app on your watch and click on **General.**
- Click on **Wake Screen,** then toggle off **Wake Screen on Wrist Raise.**

Keep the Watch Display Longer

To keep the display on longer when you click on the screen to wake your watch,

- Open the Settings app ⚙ on your watch and click on **General**.
- Click on **Wake Screen,** then click on **Wake for 70 Seconds**.

Enable Flashlight

- Press the digital crown to navigate to your watch face, then Swipe up from your watch face to open the Control Center.
- Click on the flashlight icon 🔦 . Then swipe to the left to select a flashlight mode: steady red light, flashing white light, or steady white light.
- Swipe down from the top of the watch face or press the side button or the digital crown to disable flashlight.

Note that the flashlight shines bright only when the watch is away from you. It shines at the default brightness level when you turn the watch screen to your face.

Theater Mode on Apple Watch

This feature comes in handy when in a concert, movie theater, or other public gatherings. It disables the watch display from coming on when you raise your wrist.

- Press the digital crown to navigate to your watch face, then Swipe up from your watch face to open the Control Center.
- Then click on **Theater Mode** 🎭 icon to enable it.
- Click on this same icon to disable Theater Mode.

- Press the side button or the digital crown to wake your watch when the Theater mode is enabled.

Change Brightness and Text Size

This is how to change the brightness & the text size on your watch.

- Open the Settings app on your watch and click on **Brightness & Text Size.**
- Tap the right or the left icon on the brightness scale or turn the digital crown to increase or reduce the brightness.
- Scroll down and click on **Text Size,** then tap the right or the left icon on the text size section or turn the digital crown to increase or reduce the size. You may also toggle on **Bold Text** if you need, then restart your Apple Watch.

148

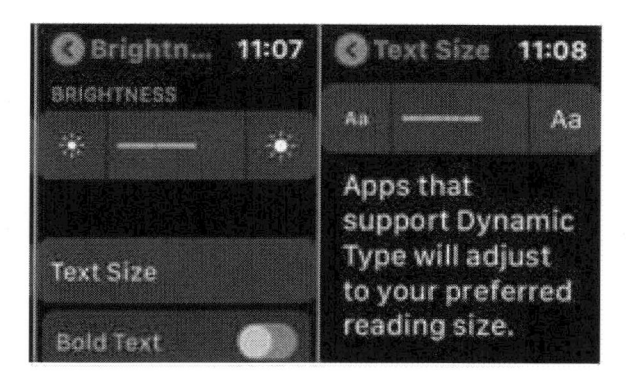

Chapter 26: Sounds and Notifications

Enable Silent Mode

To put your watch in silent mode,

- Press the digital crown to navigate to your watch face, then Swipe up from your watch face to open the Control Center.

- Then tap the 🔔 icon to activate silent mode. Click the same icon to disable.

Disable Silent Mode on Watch App

- Open the Watch app on your iPhone and click on **My Watch** at the bottom of your screen.

- Click on **Sounds & Haptics,** then enable or disable **Silent Mode.**

Mute Alerts with Your Palm

With sound enabled, you can cover your watch screen with your palm for about three seconds to mute any incoming sound. But first, you need to enable this option with the steps below:

- Open the Watch app on your iPhone and click on **My Watch** at the bottom of your screen.

- Click on **Sounds & Haptics,** then enable or disable **Cover to Mute.**

Enable Do Not Disturb

Enable this feature if you do not want alerts and incoming calls to make sounds or light up your screen.

- Press the digital crown to navigate to your watch face, then swipe up from your watch face to open the Control Center.

- Tap the 🌙 icon to activate, then select a duration: **On, On until this evening, On for 1 hour, On until end of event,** or **On until I leave.**
- Click on the same icon to disable.

Here is another way to activate this option

- Open the Settings app ⚙ on your watch and click on **Do Not Disturb.**
- Then toggle on **Do Not Disturb.**

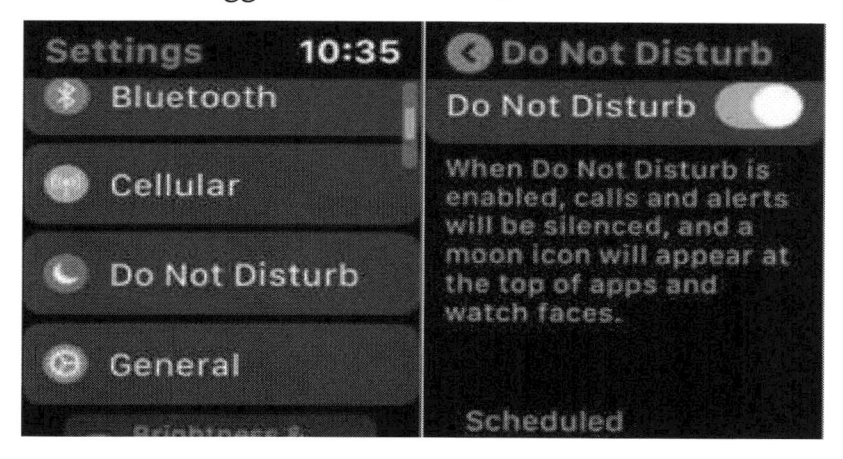

Tip: to silence the iPhone and Apple Watch at the same time, open the Watch app on your phone and click on the **My Watch** tab, then click on **General.** Click on **Do Not Disturb,** then toggle on **Mirror iPhone.** The next time you enable this feature on one device, it will automatically apply to the other device.

Set Up Notifications

Here is how to set up notifications for your watch

- Open the Watch app on your iPhone and click on **My Watch** at the bottom of your screen.
- Click on **Notifications** at the top of your screen.
- Then click on the native apps to view their notification settings.
- Click on the notification type that you want:
    - ✓ **Send to Notification Center:** to only show messages when you swipe down with your finger.
    - ✓ **Allow Notifications:** to see all the notification from the app.
    - ✓ **Notifications Off:** no notification from selected apps.

View Notifications

Whenever you have a notification, you will see a tiny red dot at the top of your watch screen. To view the notification,

- Wake your screen, then swipe down from the top to go to the notification center.
- Click on the notification to read it.
- Then click on **Clear, Dismiss,** or **Done** to remove the notification.

Clear Notifications Quickly

The steps below will show you how to delete all your notifications at the same time.

- Open the Notification Center by swiping down from the top of your screen.
- Press firmly on your screen until you see the **Clear All** screen. Then click the **X** button to delete all notification.

Hide Notifications

Here is how to hide notifications that come into your watch

- Open the Watch app on your iPhone and click on **My Watch** at the bottom of your screen.
- Click on **Notifications** at the top of your screen. You will find two setting options on the next screen: **Notification Privacy** and **Notifications Indicator**.
    - ✓ Toggle on **Notification Privacy** if you do not want to receive alert pop-ups when you have a new notification.
    - ✓ Toggle off **Notifications Indicator** to stop seeing the red dot on your watch screen that informs you of a notification.

Disable Notifications on iPhone and Apple Watch

To stop receiving notifications on your devices,

- Click on **Notifications** in the Settings app of your iPhone.
- Click on the desired app.
- Then toggle off **Allow Notifications**
- Repeat the steps above for all the needed apps.

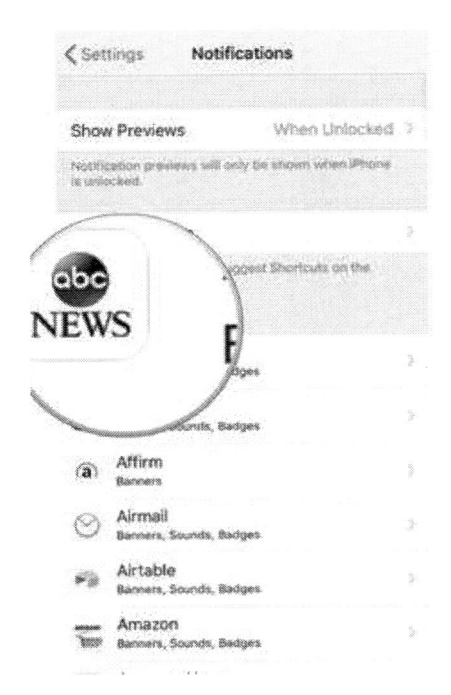

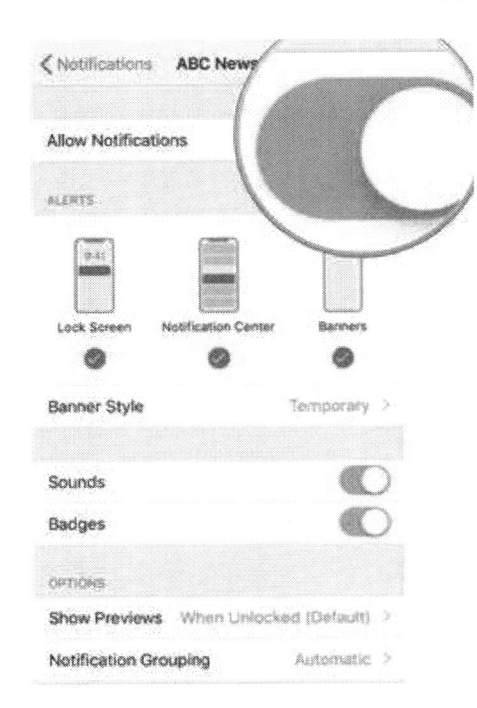

Disable Notifications for Third-Party Apps

- Open the Watch app on your iPhone and click on **My Watch** at the bottom of your screen.

- Click on **Notifications** at the top of your screen. Then toggle off the option for individual apps.

My Watch
10:09
10:09
Complications
Notifications
App Layout
Cellular

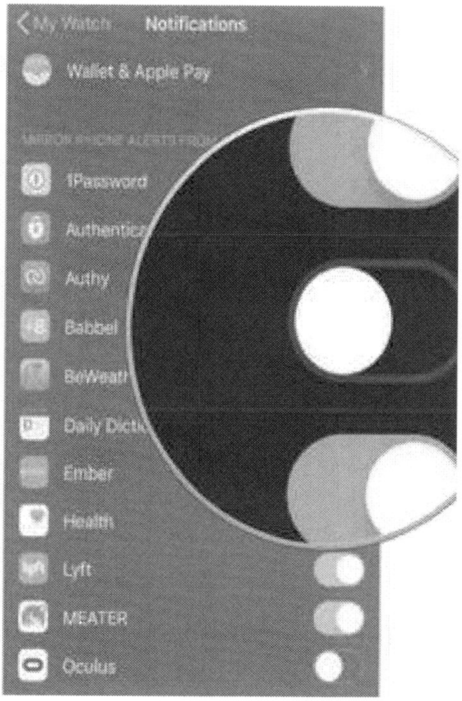

My Watch
Notifications
Wallet & Apple Pay
1Password
Authy
Babbel
Ember
Health
Lyft
MEATER
Oculus

Chapter 27: Accessibility on Apple Watch

Accessibility tool on the Apple Watch makes it easy for everyone to use the technology. For instance, persons with impaired vision can use tools like VoiceOver to navigate their watch using audio guidance. You may also need to zoom in on your screen to see better.

Set Side Button Speed

To set the response speed of your watch's side button.

- Open the Watch app on your iPhone and click on **My Watch** at the bottom of your screen.
- Click on **Accessibility,** then click on **Side Button Click Speed.**
- Select your desired speed.

Enable VoiceOver on Apple Watch

With this feature enabled, tap on your watch screen to read out what is happening on the screen. Double click on the screen to perform an action.

- Open the Settings app on your watch and click on **Accessibility.**
- Click on **VoiceOver,** then toggle on **VoiceOver.**

Enable VoiceOver Via Watch App

- Open the Watch app on your iPhone and click on **My Watch** at the bottom of your screen.
- Click on **Accessibility,** then click on **Off** by the right side of **VoiceOver.**
- Now toggle on **VoiceOver.**

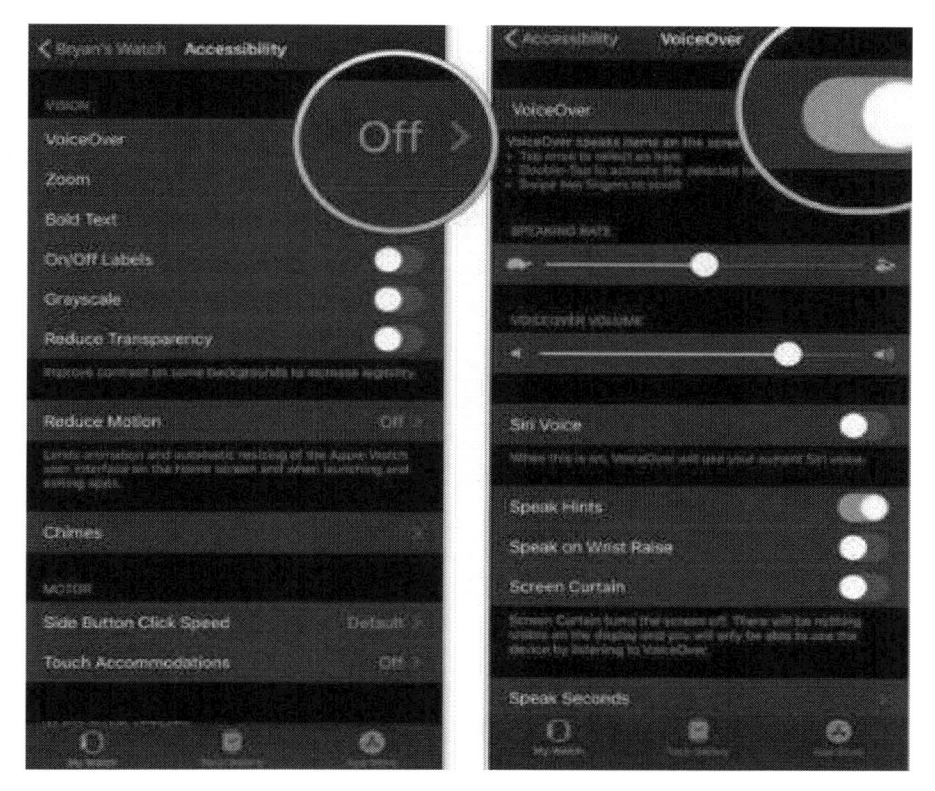

Enable Zoom on Apple Watch

Zoom allows persons who need greater visual accessibility to set a default magnification level for their watch, while also allowing them to adjust it dynamically. So, you can make small text larger & easier to see.

- Open the Settings app on your watch and click on **Accessibility.**
- Click on **Zoom,** then toggle on **Zoom.**
- Use the – or + button to decrease or increase the maximum zoom level.

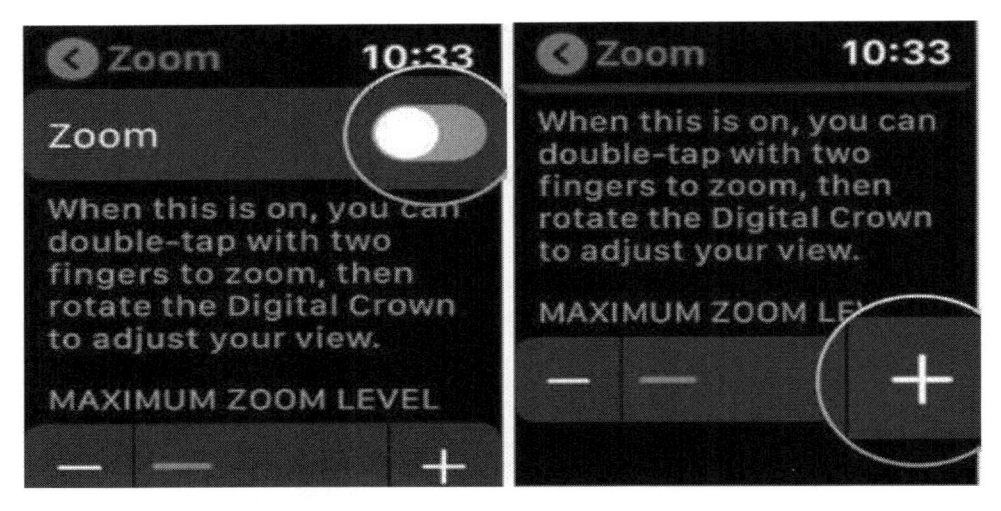

Enable Zoom Via Watch App

- Open the Watch app on your iPhone and click on the **My Watch** at the bottom of your screen.
- Click on **Accessibility,** then click on **Off** by the right side of **Zoom.**
- Now toggle on **Zoom.**
- Pull the slider to the right, or the left the modify the zoom level.

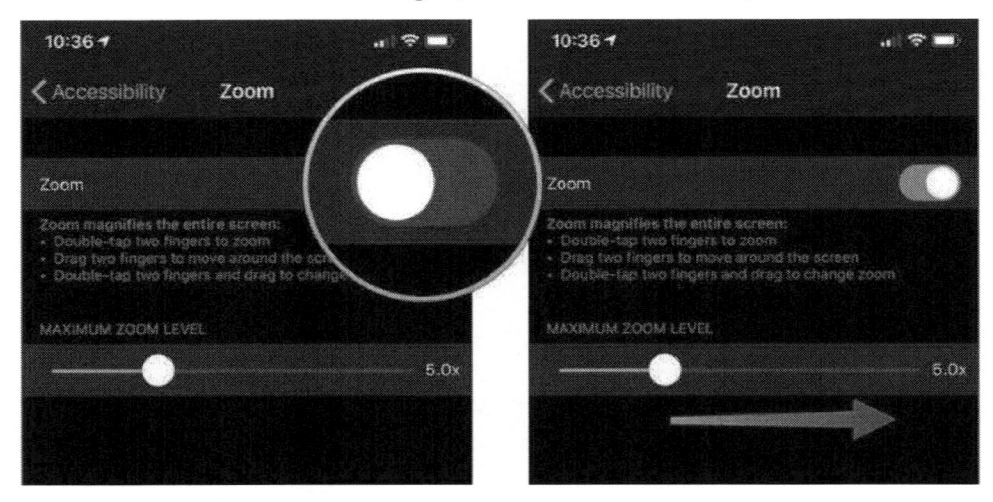

Control Zoom on Apple Watch

All you need to access zoom is to double click on your screen.

158

- Double click with your two fingers to zoom into the display on your screen.
- Double-click, hold, and drag with your two fingers to modify the degree of zoom on your device.

Customize Accessibility Shortcut

When you triple-click your watch display, it can either activate VoiceOver or Zoom. Here is how to assign a feature to triple-click.

- Open the Watch app on your iPhone and click on the **My Watch** at the bottom of your screen.
- Click on **Accessibility,** then click on **Accessibility Shortcut.**
- Then click on either **VoiceOver** or **Zoom.**

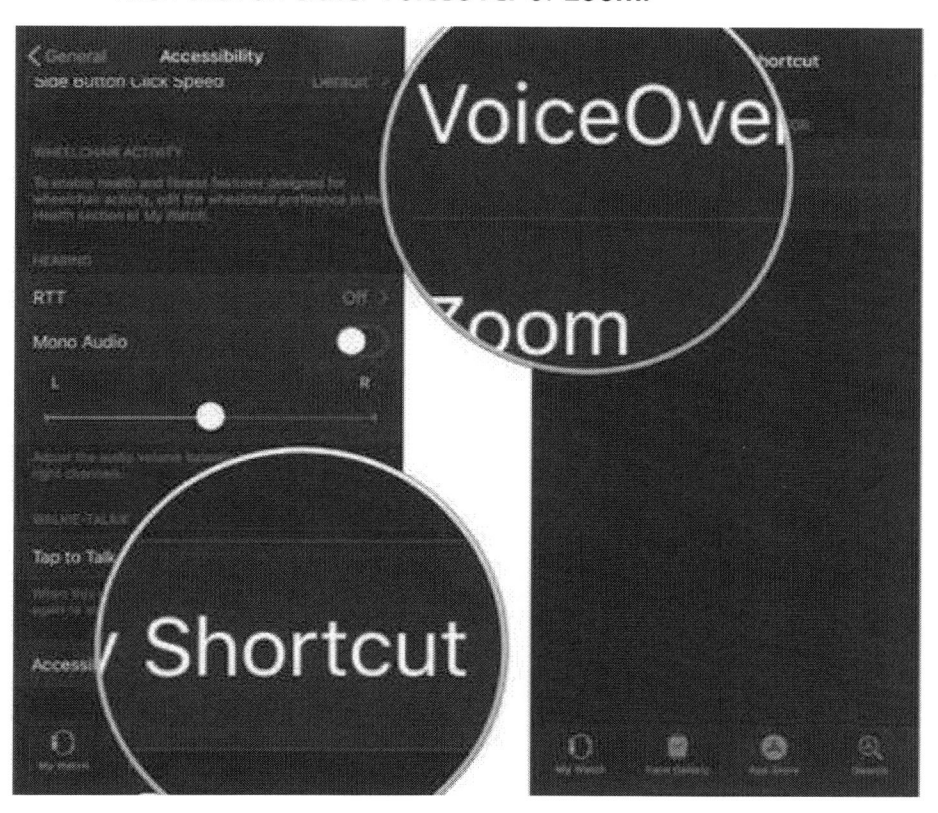

Chapter 28: Time Keeping

Set an Alarm

- Click on the Alarms app on your watch. Click on **Add Alarm**.
- Select either **PM** or **AM**, then choose the minutes or hours.
- Use the digital crown to modify, then click on **Set**.

Delete an Alarm

- Click on the Alarms app on your watch.
- Click on the alarm you wish to delete. Then click on **Delete**.

See the Same Alarms on Apple Watch and iPhone

To have the same alarm on your two devices,

- Create an alarm on your phone.
- Launch the Watch app on your phone and click on **My Watch.**
- Click on **Clock,** then toggle on **Push Alerts from iPhone.**

Disable Snooze on Apple Watch

You can set your alarm not to have the snooze option with the steps below

- Click on the Alarms app on your watch.
- Click on the desired alarm in the list of your alarms, then toggle off **Snooze.**

Chapter 29: Messages and Communication

Pre-Compose Custom Message Responses

The Apple Watch does not let you type directly, but you can compose some responses on your iPhone that you can use to respond to conversations on your watch.

- Launch the Watch app on your phone and click on **My Watch.**
- Click on **Messages.**
- Click on **Default Replies,** then click on **Add Reply** to create your own responses.
- To customize the default replies, click on **Edit** in the **Default Replies** screen, then tap ⊖ to delete a response. You can also drag the response to reorder them.

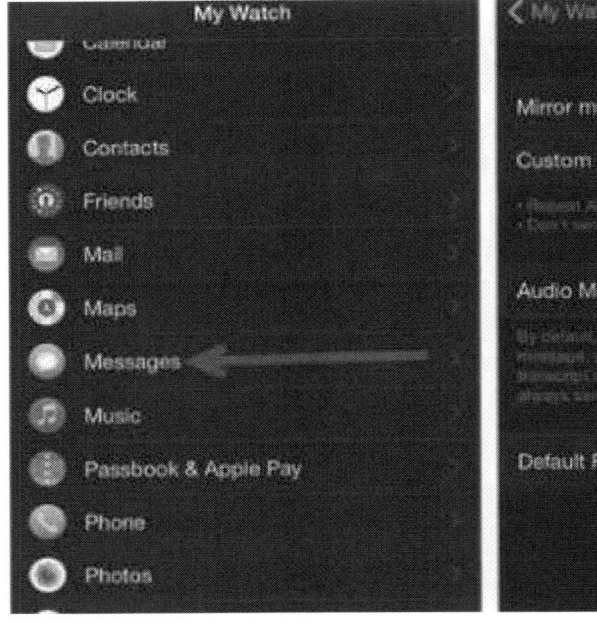

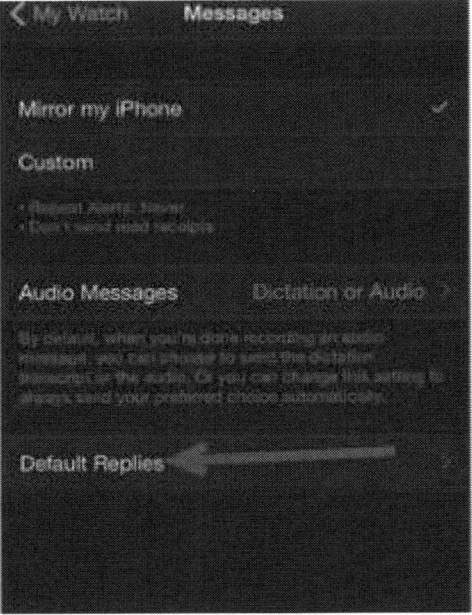

Send Dictated Text as Audio

While you can not type your response, you can speak or scribble your message. After dictating your response, your watch will ask whether you want to send the dictated text as an audio clip or as text. If you want your receiver to get your message always as an audio clip, follow the steps below to enable this

- Launch the Watch app on your phone and click on **My Watch.**
- Click on **Messages.**
- Click on **Dictated Messages.**
- Then click on **Audio** from the displayed option.

Share Your Location in Messages

Here is how to send your current location to your friends via Messages on your watch

- Open the message conversation on your watch.
- Force touch the display, then click on **Send Location.**

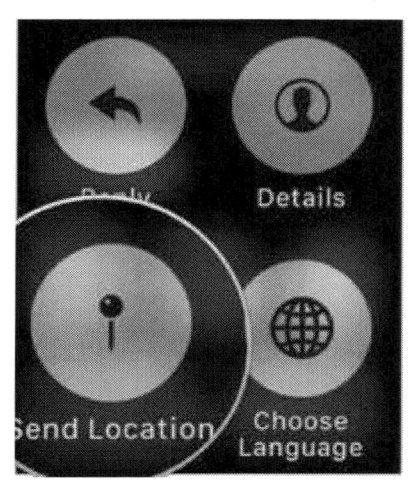

If you did not see this option, it means that you did not enable location sharing. See the steps below:

- Open the Settings app on your iPhone. Click on your name, then click on **Find My** and confirm that **Share My Location** is enabled.

- Open the Settings app on your watch, click on **privacy,** click on **Location Services,** then toggle on **Share My Location.**

Call the Person You Are Messaging

- Open the message conversation on your watch.

- Press firmly on your screen, click on **Details,** then click on .

Hold a Call Until You Can Find Your iPhone

You can use your Apple Watch to respond to incoming calls on your iPhone. If you prefer to attend to the call on your iPhone, click on **Answer on iPhone** to put the call on hold until you reach your iPhone. The caller will hear a short sound until you answer the call on your iPhone.

Send Money With Apple Pay

- Open the Messages app on your watch and click on an existing conversation or begin a new one.

- Click on .

- Use your digital crown to choose the amount, then click on **Pay.**

- Confirm your action, then click the side button twice to send.

Cancel a Payment

You can cancel a payment only if the recipient is yet to accept it.

- Launch the Watch app on your phone and click on **My Watch.**
- Click on **Wallet & Apple Pay,** then click on your Apple Cash card.
- Click on **Transactions,** click on the transaction, then click on **Cancel Payment.**

Request a Payment

- Use the virtual assistant to request a payment. This will open the Message app on your watch to display your payment request. Click on **Request.**

Respond to Payment Request

When you receive a payment request, follow the steps below to accept and pay

- Open the payment request in the messages app on your watch and click on **Pay.**
- Tap buttons or use the digital crown to change the amount, if necessary. Click on **Pay,** then tap the side button twice to complete.

Create a Message on Apple Watch

- Launch the Message app on your watch. Press firmly on your screen, then click on **New Message.**
- Click on **Add Contact,** click on a contact in the list on your screen, then select any of the displayed options:
    - ✓ Click on to select from your complete contact list.

✓ Click on ⊞ to input a phone number.

✓ Click on 🎤 to dictate a phone number or search for a contact.

Reply to a Message

- Use the digital crown to move to the bottom of the message, then click on any of the displayed options to send your reply.

Dictate your response.

Scroll to see more smart replies.

Send a digital touch.

- To respond with a smiley, double click on the message, then click on a smiley, like a heart, thumbs-down, or a thumbs-up.

Scribble a Message

- Open the Messages app ⭕ on your watch and click on an existing conversation or press firmly on your screen, then click on **New Message.**

- Click on+ , then start to write your message. While you scribble, use the digital crown to see predictive text options, click on the correct one to select it.
- Click on **Send** once done.

Send Emoji

- Open the Messages app on your watch and click on an existing conversation or press firmly on your screen, then click on **New Message.**
- Click on , click on a category then swipe through the available images. Click on an emoji to send it.

Send Animoji/ Memoji in the Messages App

To send an Animoji,

- Open the Messages app on your watch and click on an existing conversation or press firmly on your screen, then click on **New Message.**
- Click on , swipe past the standard emoji, till you get to an Animoji. Click on the Animoji to send.
- Scroll to the end of your screen and click on **More Stickers** to see all the Memoji. Click on the one you desire to send it.

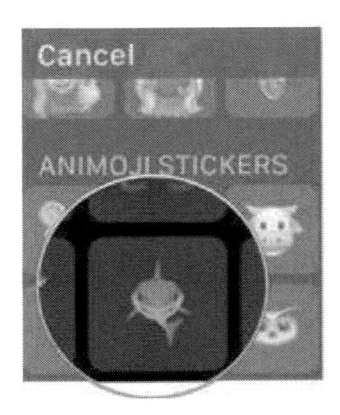

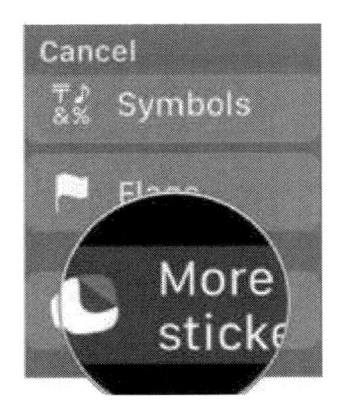

Choose the Mailboxes that Should Appear on Your Watch

Assuming you have more than one email address and you do not want to receive notifications and information from all the addresses, follow the steps to select a specific mailbox for your watch.

- Launch the Watch app on your phone and click on **My Watch.**
- Click on **Mail,** click on **Include Mail.**
- Navigate to **Accounts** and click on the mailboxes that should apply.

To configure this setting from your Apple watch,

- Open the Mail app on your watch.
- Swipe down and click on **Edit.**
- Then click on a mailbox or an account to include it.

Flag a Mail

If you received an email and wish to respond to it later on your phone, or computer, follow the steps below to flag the mail.

- Open the Mail app on your watch.
- Press firmly on your screen, then click on **Flag.**

Chapter 30: The Dock on your Apple Watch

The dock on your Watch displays shortcuts to your favorite apps or your recently opened apps. You can use it to quickly access apps or to control your music.

Use Dock to Switch Between Apps

See below how to use the dock to access your apps:
- Press the side button of your watch.
- Swipe or turn the digital crown to view your apps.
- Click on an app to open it.
- Scroll to the end of the dock screen and tap **All Apps** to go to your home screen.
- Press the side button to exit the dock.

Select Apps that Should Appear in the Dock

You have two options when it comes to using the dock on your watch. You can either show up to ten of your favorite apps or show your most recent apps. The Favorites app option allows you to add the apps that you like while the Recents option will show your recently used apps in the order that you opened them. Follow the steps below to choose between Favorites and Recents.
- Open the Watch app on your iPhone and click on the **My Watch** at the bottom of your screen.
- Click on **Dock,** then select either **Favorites** or **Recents.**

Add Favorite Apps to the Dock

If you selected the Favorites option, follow the steps below to add up to ten of your favorite apps to the dock:

- Launch the Watch app on your phone and click on **My Watch.**
- Click on **Dock.** Check that **Favorites** is selected.
- Click on **Edit.** Tap ⊖ to remove an app, then tap **Remove.**
- Go to the **Do Not Include** and click the plus icon ⊕ beside an app to add it to your favorite.

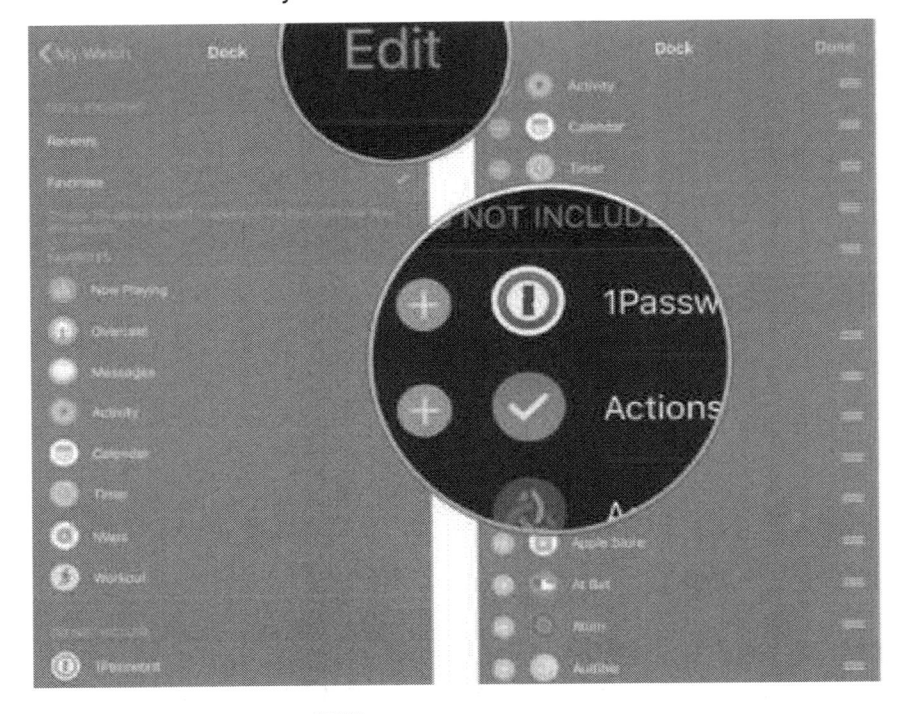

- Touch & hold ☰ beside an app to change the location on the dock.
- Tap **Done** to accept the changes.

Add Apps to Your Watch Dock

When using this feature in the Recents mode, you will see that the apps are added in the order that you open them, the most recent being on top. If using the Favorite option, the only way you can add apps directly on your Apple Watch is if you recently opened the app and if you do not have up to ten apps. If all these are met, follow the steps below to add the most recently opened app

- Press the side button, then swipe to the top of the dock list.
- Stay on the top card for a while until the card expands under the **Recent** heading.
- Click on **Keep in Dock** to add the app.

Rearrange Apps in Your Dock

- Launch the Watch app on your phone and click on **My Watch.**
- Click on **Dock.**
- Click on **Edit** at the top right side of your screen.
- Drag the ☰ icon beside the app you want to move and drag it to your desired position.
- Click on **Done** to save your changes.

Remove Apps From Your Dock

You can do this directly on your Apple Watch, or your iPhone.

- Launch the Watch app on your phone and click on **My Watch**.
- Click on **Dock**.
- Click on **Edit** at the top right side of your screen.
- Click the ⊖ icon beside the app you want to remove, then tap **Remove** and tap **Done** to confirm.

On Apple Watch

- Press the side button, then swipe to the app you wish to delete.
- Swipe left on the app, then click the red delete icon.

Chapter 31: Water Lock Mode

The Apple Watch can stay in up to 50 meters of water. However, you need to activate Water Lock mode before you wear your watch in water. When you come out of the water, use the digital crown to dispel the water from your watch.

Enable Water Lock

- Press the digital crown to go to the watch face.
- Go to the Control Center – swipe up from the bottom of your screen. From other screens, press down the bottom of your watch screen, then swipe up.
- Click on the Water Lock icon to enable it. Click on this same icon to disable the water lock.

Eject Water

To eject water from your watch after a dip,

- Rotate the digital crown until your screen reads **"Unlocked."**

- You will hear a series of tones play as you move the digital crown. You will also see an animation on your watch screen to confirm that the water is cleared from the speaker, and the process is complete.

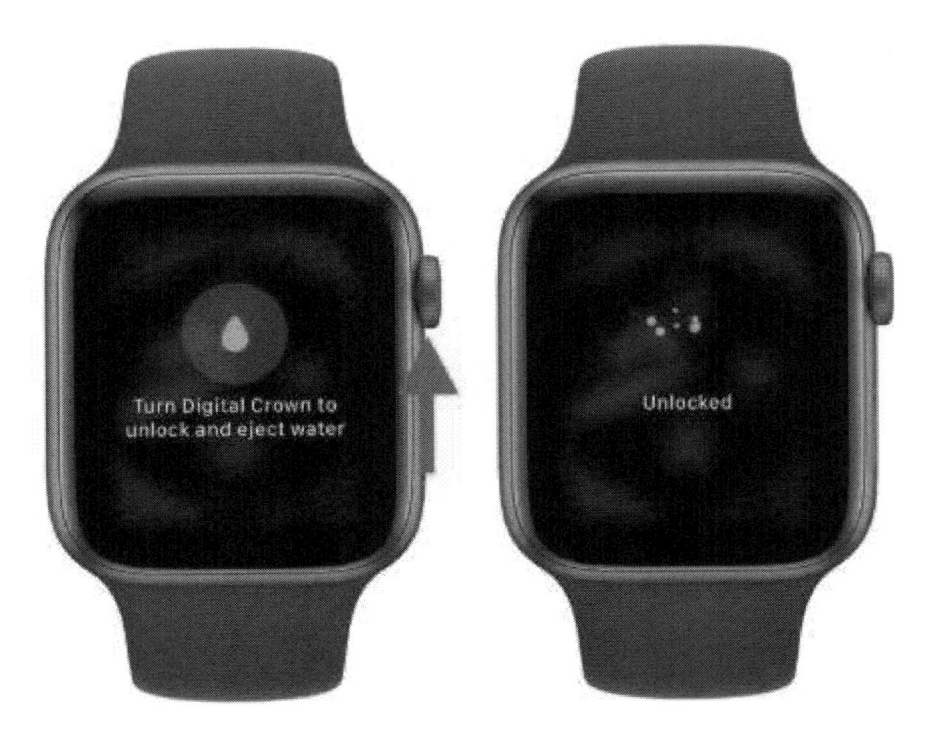

Chapter 32: Free Up Space on Your Watch

The Apple Watch, just like other similar gadgets, has limited storage space. If you experience space constraints on your watch, you can delete contents and apps that you do not use. Let us look at how to create space on your device. You can view your available watch space, as well as see the amount of space used by each content and apps so that you can quickly tell what is eating your device space.

Check Storage Space on Apple Watch

Here is how to tell the available storage space on your watch, using your Apple Watch:

- Launch the Settings app on your watch.
- Click on **General,** then click on **Usage.**
- On the screen, you will view your available storage space as well as used space.
- Swipe down to see the amount of space that each content and app used.

Check Storage Space on iPhone

Here is how to tell the available storage space on your watch, using your paired iPhone:

- Launch the Watch app on your phone and click on **My Watch** at the bottom of your screen. Then click on **General**
- On the next screen, click on **About,** and you will view the total number of photos, songs, and other applications on the watch. You will also see the available space on your watch.

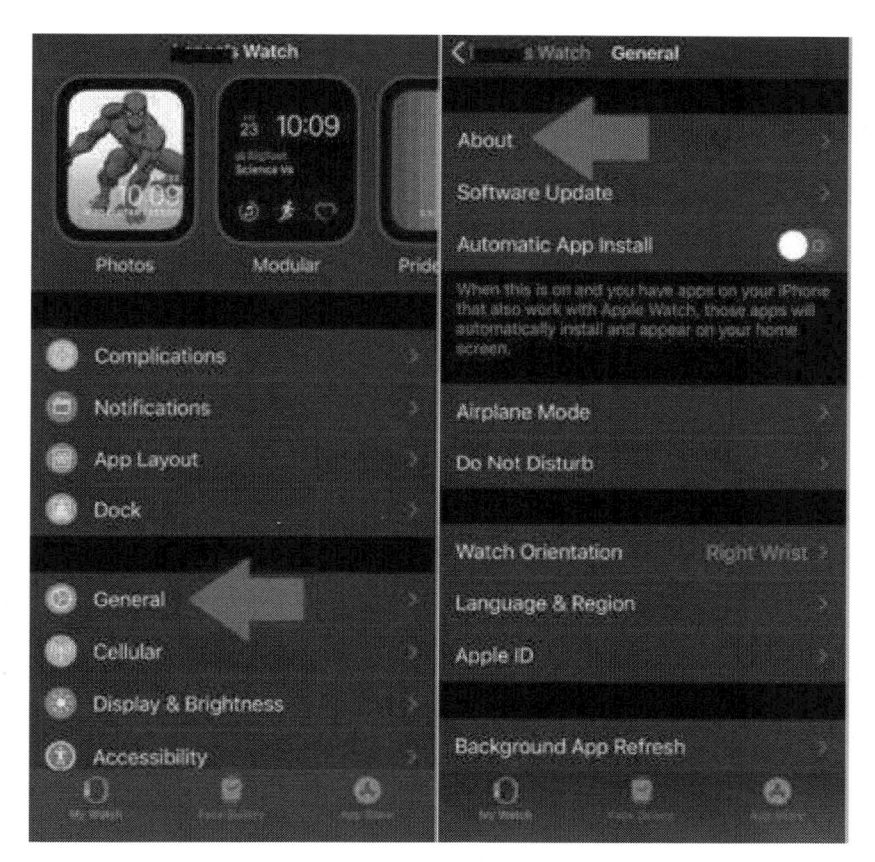

Remove Apps From Watch App

After you discover the apps taking up space on your watch, follow the steps below to delete the apps via the Watch app on your iPhone.

- Launch the Watch app on your phone and swipe down till you get to the **Installed on Apple Watch** section.
- Click on the app that you wish to delete.
- Toggle off **Show App on Apple Watch** to delete the app from your watch.
- To install the app again, go to the **Available Apps** section of the Watch app and click the Install button for the app.

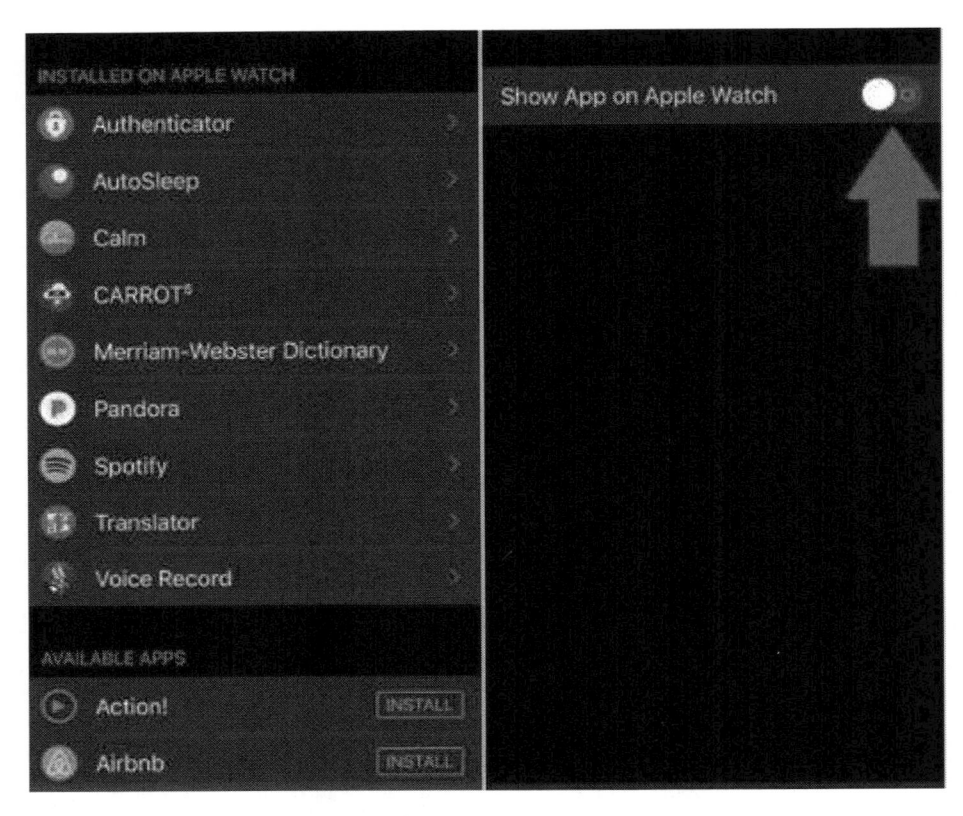

Delete Apps on Apple Watch

Here is how to delete apps directly on the Apple Watch.

- Press the digital crown to go to your home screen.
- If your home screen is in Grid view, gently press down on any of the app icons until they begin to wiggle, then click on the **X** button above the app that you want to delete. Then click on the Delete icon to remove the app. Press the Digital Crown to escape the wiggle mode.
- If your watch's home screen is in **List View,** swipe down to the app you want to delete, then swipe left on the app. Click on the trash can icon. Then click on **Delete App.**

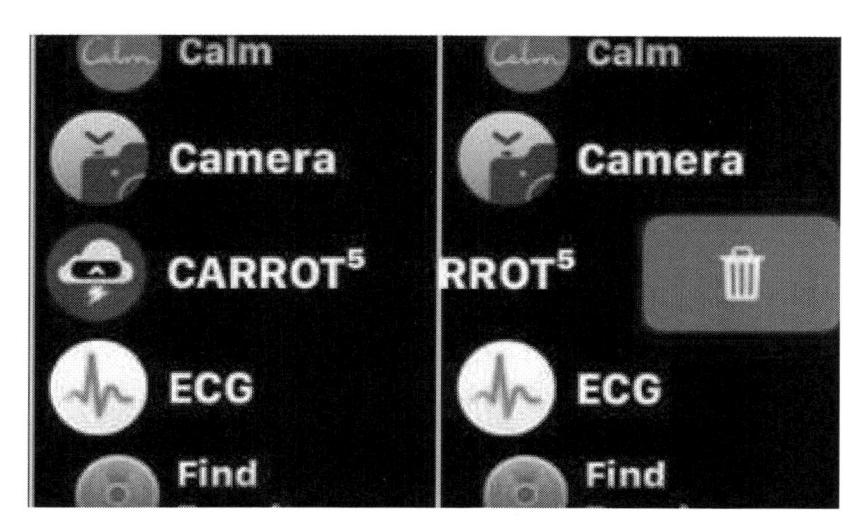

Remove Music From Watch App

Here is how to delete music from your watch

- Open the Watch app on your phone, click on the **My Watch** tab, then click on **Music.**

- Tap **Edit** at the top of your screen, then tap the ⊖ icon beside the album or playlist.

- Then click on **Delete,** and tap **Done** to escape this view.

- On the Music screen, you may toggle on **Heavy Rotation** if you want to download playlists and albums that you play on your phone. Toggle off the option to remove your recent albums.

Delete Music on Apple Watch

Here is how to delete music on your Apple Watch

- Launch the Music app on your Apple Watch.
- Scroll down on the album thumbnail until you get to the option for **Library** and **On iPhone.** Click on **Library,** then click on **Albums.**
- Scroll down to the album you want to delete. Then swipe left on the album and click on the ••• icon.

- Tap **Remove,** then click on **Remove Download** to remove the album from your Apple Watch.

Resync Photos from Watch App

This option allows you to limit or change the photos that should be synced from your phone to your watch.

- Open the Watch app on your phone, click on the **My Watch** tab, then click on **Photos.**
- You have the option to choose **Custom** or **Mirror Your iPhone.** Tap the option that suits you, then scroll down and click on **Synced Album.**
- Choose another album, like one that contains fewer photos.
- Return to the previous screen, and click on **Photos Limit.** Then reduce the number of synced photos. Your watch will automatically update the synced photos.

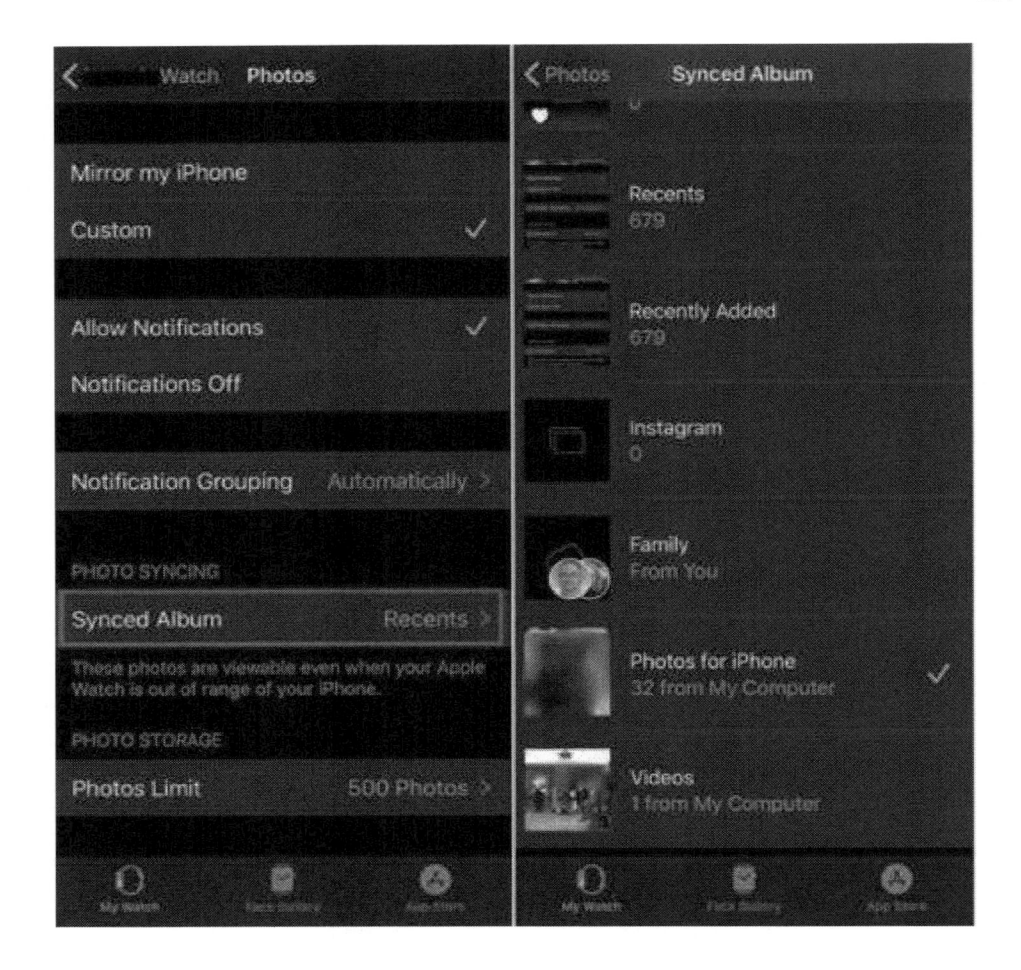

Remove Audiobooks

Here is how to delete audiobooks from your watch

- Open the Watch app on your phone, click on the **My Watch** tab, then click on **Audiobooks** to view a variety of options.
- Toggle off **Want to Read** and **Reading Now.** Then scroll through the audiobooks to find the ones you no longer want. Swipe left on the audiobook, then tap **Delete.**

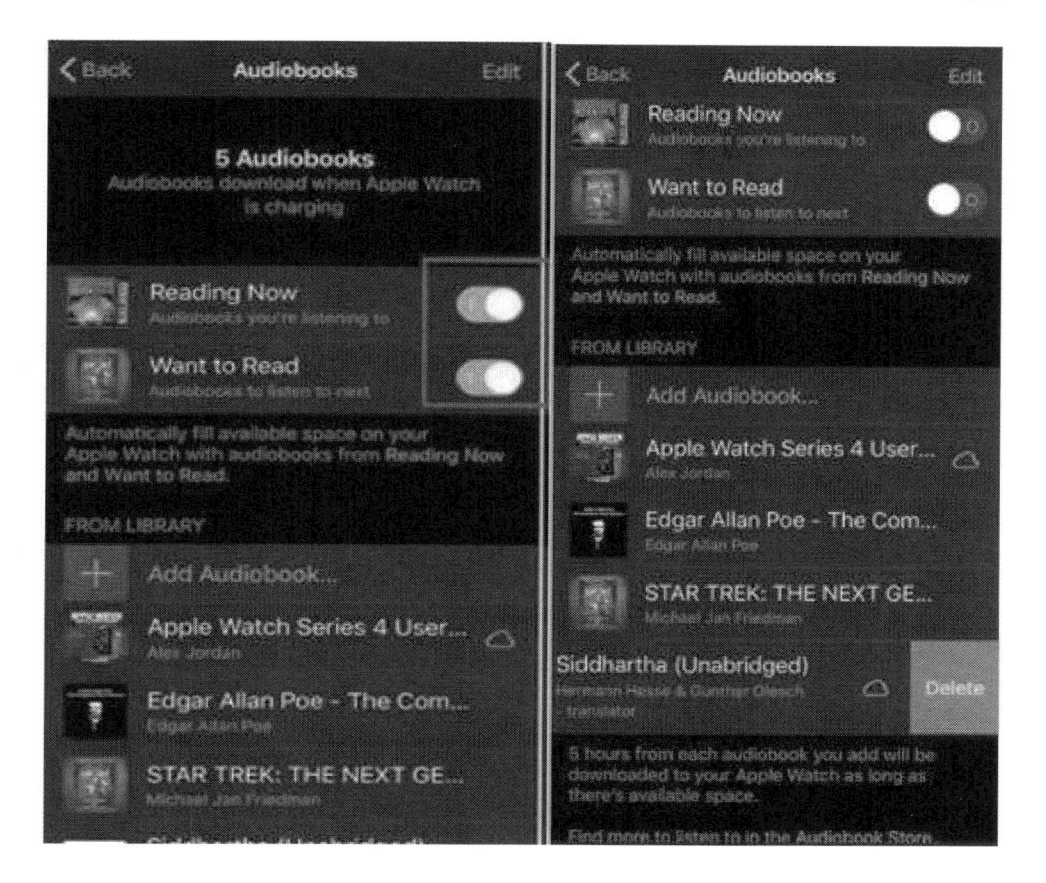

Remove Podcasts

Here is how to delete podcasts from your watch

- Open the Watch app on your phone, click on the **My Watch** tab, then click on **Podcasts** to view the available options.
- Under **Add Episodes From,** select either **Custom** or **Listen Now. Listen Now** downloads one episode from the top ten podcasts that you listen to while the **Custom** option downloads three episodes from selected shows.

- Then toggle off any podcasts that you do not want on your Apple Watch.

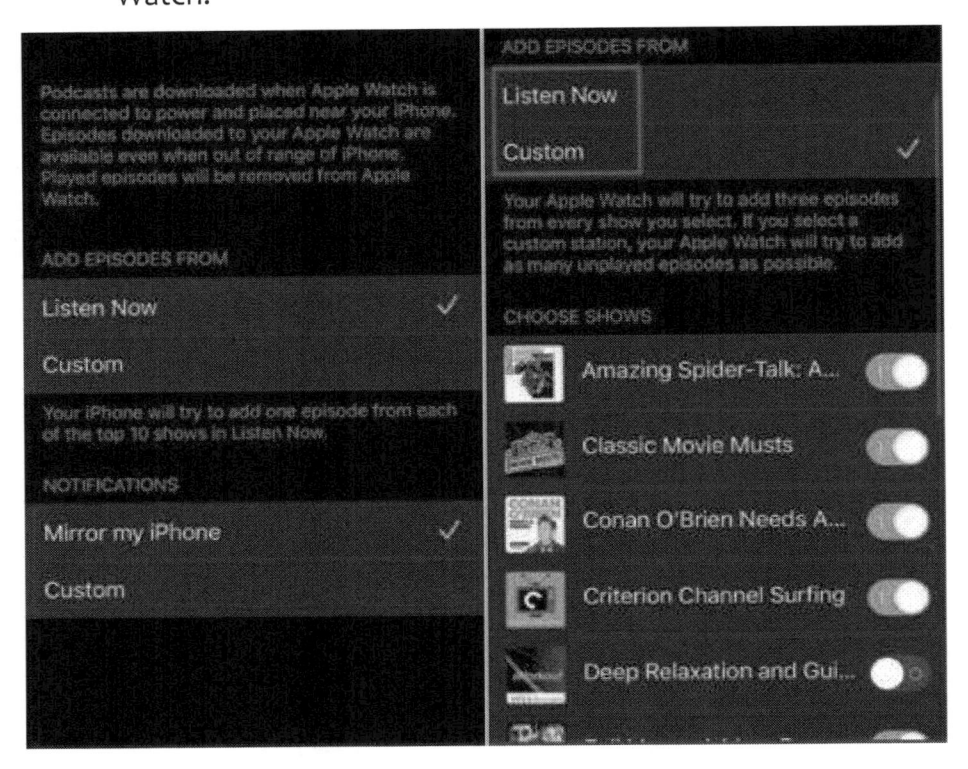

Chapter 33: Battery Tips

Enable Power Reserve Mode

Activate this feature if you need to prolong the battery life of your watch.

- Swipe up from your watch face to access the Control Center.
- Click on the battery percentage, then drag the **Power Reserve** slider to the right to enable.
- Click on **Proceed** to complete.

Disable Power Reserve Mode

- Press the side button until the Apple logo shows up on your screen. Then allow your watch to reboot completely.

Check Battery Percentage

To see your battery percentage,

- Swipe up from your watch face to access the Control Center.
- You will see your battery percent on the next screen.

Conclusion

Thank you for purchasing this book. I have included all that you need to know to get the best results from your smartwatch. I will also like to read from you. Please leave me a review on Amazon if you find this book helpful.

Thank you.

Other Books By Nobert Young

- Samsung Galaxy S20 User Guide for Beginners
  https://www.amazon.com/dp/B085DRDXJZ
- Samsung Galaxy Note 20 User Guide
  https://www.amazon.com/dp/B08G54JN8G
- DeepFake Technology: Complete Guide to Deepfakes, Politics and Social Media https://amzn.to/2LddlFk
- Senior's Guide to the Samsung Galaxy S20
  https://www.amazon.com/dp/B085R6JM1G
- Senior's Guide to the Samsung Galaxy Note 20
  https://www.amazon.com/dp/B08G571T5H
- Apple TV App User Guide
  https://www.amazon.com/dp/B07ZN8J1B3
- Beginner's Guide To The Apple Airpods Pro
  https://www.amazon.com/dp/1704860962
- Senior's Guide To The Apple Airpods Pro
  https://www.amazon.com/dp/B07ZXY29DF

Printed in Great Britain
by Amazon